# Colombia Travel Guide

Discover the Natural Wonders, Rich History, and Vibrant Culture of South America's Hidden Heart. Pocket Edition

## Pablo Cardenas

© Copyright 2025 by Pablo Cardenas
All rights reserved

This document is geared towards providing exact and reliable information with regards to the topic and issue covered. The publication is sold with the idea that the publisher is not required to render accounting, officially permitted, or otherwise, qualified services. If advice is necessary, legal or professional, a practiced individual in the profession should be ordered.

From a Declaration of Principles which was accepted and approved equally by a Committee of the American Bar Association and a Committee of Publishers and Associations.

In no way is it legal to reproduce, duplicate, or transmit any part of this document in either electronic means or in printed format. Recording of this publication is strictly prohibited and any storage of this document is not allowed unless with written permission from the publisher. All rights reserved.

The information provided herein is stated to be truthful and consistent, in that any liability, in terms of inattention or otherwise, by any usage or abuse of any policies, processes, or directions contained within is the solitary and utter responsibility of the recipient reader. Under no circumstances will any legal responsibility or blame be held against the publisher for any reparation, damages, or monetary loss due to the information herein, either directly or indirectly.

Respective authors own all copyrights not held by the publisher.

The information herein is offered for informational purposes solely, and is universal as so. The presentation of the information is without contract or any type of guarantee assurance.

The trademarks that are used are without any consent, and the publication of the trademark is without permission or backing by the trademark owner. All trademarks and brands within this book are for clarifying purposes only and are the owned by the owners themselves, not affiliated with this document.

# TABLE OF CONTENTS

*Introduction ........................................................................ 8*

    Why Colombia Is South America's Hidden Heart............................ 8

    How to Use This Guide ................................................................ 12

    Must-Know Facts About Colombia: Geography, Climate, and People 16

    A Brief History of Colombia: From Ancient Civilizations to Modern Times ........................................................................................... 20

*Chapter 1: Colombia's Vibrant Cities............................................. 25*

    Bogotá: The Capital's Cultural and Historical Treasures ................... 25

    Medellín: The City of Eternal Spring................................................ 28

    Cartagena: A Caribbean Jewel Steeped in History........................... 32

    Cali: Salsa, Nightlife, and Afro-Colombian Culture .......................... 35

    Barranquilla: Carnival and Coastal Charm....................................... 39

    Santa Marta: Gateway to Tayrona National Park............................. 42

    Bucaramanga: The City of Parks and Adventure ............................. 46

    Popayán: Colombia's White City of Colonial Elegance..................... 50

    Pereira and Manizales: Discovering the Coffee Triangle's Urban Gems ....................................................................................................... 53

*Chapter 2: Exploring Colombia's Natural Wonders ...................... 59*

    Tayrona National Park: Beaches, Jungle, and Adventure ................. 59

    The Amazon Rainforest: A Journey into Biodiversity........................ 62

    The Cocora Valley: Home of the World's Tallest Palm Trees ........... 66

    The Guajira Peninsula: Desert Landscapes and Indigenous Culture .. 70

    Caño Cristales: The River of Five Colors .......................................... 73

    Los Nevados National Park: Hiking in the Andes ............................. 77

    San Andrés and Providencia: Colombia's Island Paradise................. 81

    Chicamocha Canyon: Colombia's Grand Canyon ............................. 84

## Chapter 3: Colombia's Rich History and Culture ........................... 90

Pre-Colombian Civilizations: From the Muisca to the Tairona .......... 90

The Spanish Conquest and Colonial Era ............................................... 94

Independence and the Birth of Modern Colombia .............................. 98

The Impact of Coffee: Colombia's Role in the Coffee Trade ............ 101

Music and Dance: Cumbia, Salsa, and Vallenato .............................. 106

Celebrations and Festivals: Carnival, Feria de las Flores, and More. 109

Indigenous Cultures: Preserving Traditions in a Modern World ...... 113

## Chapter 4: Culinary Delights of Colombia ................................... 119

Regional Flavors: From the Caribbean Coast to the Andes .............. 119

Must-Try Dishes: Arepas, Bandeja Paisa, and Ajiaco ....................... 123

Coffee Culture: From Bean to Cup in the Coffee Triangle ................ 126

Street Food Adventures: Empanadas, Buñuelos, and More ............ 130

Drinks to Savor: Aguardiente, Lulo Juice, and Colombian Craft Beer
................................................................................................................ 134

## Chapter 5: Adventure Activities and Outdoor Experiences ........ 139

Hiking and Trekking: Discovering Colombia's Trails ........................ 139

Scuba Diving and Snorkeling in Caribbean Waters .......................... 143

Paragliding Over the Chicamocha Canyon ....................................... 147

Whitewater Rafting and Kayaking on Colombia's Rivers ................. 151

Birdwatching: Exploring the World's Most Diverse Avian Life ......... 155

Cycling and Mountain Biking Across Colombia's Landscapes .......... 159

## Chapter 6: Hidden Gems and Off-the-Beaten-Path Destinations 165

San Agustín Archaeological Park: Ancient Statues and Mysteries ... 165

Villa de Leyva: Colombia's Colonial Time Capsule ........................... 169

Mompox: A Riverside Town Frozen in Time ..................................... 172

The Tatacoa Desert: Stargazing and Unique Landscapes ................ 176

Guatapé and the Rock of El Peñol: A Day Trip from Medellín ......... 180

The Pacific Coast: Whale Watching and Untouched Beaches ......... 184
Tierradentro: Colombia's Underground Tombs............................. 187
Jardín: A Coffee Town with Vibrant Colors...................................... 191
Leticia: Gateway to the Amazon ..................................................... 195

*Conclusion*............................................................................................ *200*

Recap: Why Colombia Should Be Your Next Adventure ................. 200

*BONUS 1: Printable travel journal* ............................................ *204*

*BONUS 2: 10 tips "that can save the day" on your trip in Colombia* ................................................................................................. *205*

*BONUS 3: Essential phrases for your daily travel needs in Colombia* ................................................................................................. *206*

# INTRODUCTION

## Why Colombia Is South America's Hidden Heart

Colombia stands as a country of profound contrasts and unparalleled diversity, earning its title as South America's hidden heart. It is a land where the Andes splinter into three dramatic mountain ranges, carving out valleys that cradle bustling cities, fertile plains, and quaint villages. To the north, the Caribbean coastline shimmers with turquoise waters and golden sands, while the Pacific Coast offers rugged beauty and untamed wilderness. The Amazon rainforest blankets the country's southeastern expanse, teeming with biodiversity that rivals any ecosystem on Earth. This fusion of geographical marvels, cultural richness, and historical depth creates a nation that is both a crossroads and a treasure chest, waiting to be discovered.

What makes Colombia particularly unique is its position as a meeting point of worlds. Here, South America's diverse regions converge in a way that is both geographical and cultural. Its mountains, plains, jungles, deserts, and islands form a microcosm of the continent itself. This geographical diversity fosters an incredible variety of ecosystems, from páramos—high-altitude moorlands shrouded in mist—to tropical rainforests alive with the calls of macaws and howler monkeys. Colombia's natural landscapes are not merely scenic backdrops but vital, living entities that have shaped the lives and traditions of its people for centuries. The Andes, for instance, are not just a mountain range but the lifeblood of communities that rely on their fertile soil for coffee, cacao, and tropical fruits. The Amazon is not simply a jungle but a spiritual and cultural cornerstone for indigenous tribes who regard it as a living, breathing entity.

The cultural fabric of Colombia is as intricate as its landscapes. The country's history has been shaped by the intersection of indigenous, African, and European influences, creating a cultural tapestry that is as vibrant as it is complex. Cities like Cartagena and Santa Marta stand as testaments to its colonial past, with cobblestone streets and ornate cathedrals whispering stories of Spanish conquest and resilience. Meanwhile, regions like the Pacific Coast maintain strong African influences, evident in their music, food, and festivals. Indigenous cultures persist strongly in the Guajira Peninsula, the Amazon, and the Sierra Nevada de Santa Marta, where traditions have been passed down through generations despite centuries of colonization and modernization. This cultural fusion is not static; it is alive and ever-evolving, manifesting in everything from Bogotá's cutting-edge art galleries to Medellín's innovative social projects.

Colombia's rich history lends a profound sense of depth to its identity. Before the arrival of the Spanish, the land was home to advanced pre-Colombian civilizations such as the Muisca and the Tairona, whose goldwork and artifacts continue to awe historians and visitors alike. The Spanish conquest brought its own blend of tragedy and transformation, as well as the architecture and Catholic traditions that now define much of the country's visual and spiritual landscape. The struggle for independence in the early 19th century gave birth to a resilient and spirited nation, one determined to forge its destiny despite political upheavals and internal conflicts that have tested its mettle for decades. Today, Colombia stands as a testament to the power of renewal, having emerged from its turbulent history with a newfound sense of purpose and pride.

One of the most compelling reasons Colombia is considered South America's hidden heart lies in its people. Colombians are renowned for their warmth, resilience, and zest for life. Hospitality is not merely a gesture but a deeply ingrained cultural value, and visitors are often struck by the genuine kindness and generosity they encounter. Whether it's a coffee farmer in the lush hills of the Coffee Triangle inviting you to share a freshly brewed cup, or a street vendor in Cartagena offering a smile along with their wares, the human connections formed here leave an indelible mark. This warmth is matched by an infectious energy, evident in the nation's love for music, dance, and celebration. Festivals like Barranquilla's Carnival and Medellín's Feria de las Flores are not mere events but expressions of a collective passion for life that is impossible to resist.

Colombia's gastronomy further underscores its role as South America's hidden heart. The country's culinary traditions are as diverse as its landscapes, with each region offering a distinct palate of flavors and dishes. On the Caribbean coast, the cuisine reflects the influence of African and indigenous traditions, with dishes like coconut rice, fried fish, and patacones (fried plantains) taking center stage. In the Andean region, hearty staples like ajiaco, a chicken and potato stew, provide comfort against the cool mountain air. The Coffee Triangle offers not only some of the world's finest coffee but also an array of tropical fruits that seem almost otherworldly in their variety and sweetness. Street food, from arepas to empanadas, showcases the creativity and resourcefulness of Colombian cooking, turning simple ingredients into culinary delights. This gastronomic diversity mirrors the country's broader cultural and geographic richness, offering a literal taste of its multifaceted identity.

What truly sets Colombia apart is its ability to surprise. For decades, the country was overshadowed by its reputation for violence and instability, a narrative that painted it as a place best avoided. Yet Colombia has undergone a remarkable transformation in recent years, emerging as a beacon of hope and resilience. The country's cities have reinvented themselves, with Medellín in particular serving as a global model for urban innovation and social progress. Once plagued by cartel violence, the "City of Eternal Spring" is now celebrated for its modern public transportation systems, green spaces, and community-focused initiatives. Bogotá, the nation's capital, has become a cultural and artistic hub, boasting world-class museums, vibrant street art, and a thriving culinary scene. Cartagena, with its beautifully preserved colonial architecture, now attracts travelers from around the globe eager to immerse themselves in its history and coastal allure.

The element of surprise extends beyond the cities and into Colombia's natural landscapes. Visitors to Tayrona National Park, for instance, often find themselves awestruck by the juxtaposition of pristine beaches, dense jungle, and towering Sierra Nevada mountains. The Caño Cristales, known as the "River of Five Colors," defies belief with its vibrant hues, a natural phenomenon caused by a rare aquatic plant. Even the deserts of the Guajira Peninsula and the Tatacoa Desert offer unexpected beauty, their stark landscapes contrasting sharply with the lushness found elsewhere in the country. These hidden gems underscore Colombia's ability to defy expectations, offering experiences that are as diverse as they are unforgettable.

Colombia's role as South America's hidden heart is also evident in its spirit of innovation and forward momentum. The country has embraced sustainable tourism, recognizing the importance of preserving its natural and cultural treasures for future generations. Efforts to protect biodiversity, support indigenous communities, and promote eco-friendly travel are not merely trends but commitments that reflect a deeper understanding of what makes Colombia special. This forward-thinking approach is a testament to the resilience and adaptability of its people, who have turned challenges into opportunities and created a vision for the future that is as inspiring as it is ambitious.

To truly understand why Colombia is South America's hidden heart, one must experience it firsthand. It is a country that defies categorization, where every region, every city, and every community offers something distinct yet intrinsically connected to the whole. It is a land of contrasts and connections, of ancient traditions and modern innovations, of breathtaking landscapes and vibrant cultures. Above all, it is a place where the heart of South America beats strongest, inviting the world to discover its rhythm.

# How to Use This Guide

This guide has been designed to serve as a practical companion for exploring one of South America's most dynamic and multifaceted countries. Whether you're a seasoned traveler or embarking on your first journey to Colombia, the structure and content are crafted to ensure you can navigate its complexities with ease. The guide is divided into thematic chapters, each addressing a specific aspect of Colombia's geography, culture, history, and attractions. Understanding how to use the guide effectively can make your travel planning seamless and enrich your experience once you arrive.

Before diving into the specifics of the chapters, it's important to know how the information has been organized. Each section has been written with a focus on clarity and detail, aiming to balance inspiration with practicality. For example, when discussing travel tips or must-know facts, the content is geared toward providing you with actionable advice rather than overwhelming you with abstract details. Similarly, the chapters dedicated to cities, natural wonders, and cultural experiences include descriptions, key highlights, and unique characteristics to help you decide what aligns with your interests and priorities. Think of the guide as a toolbox: you can pick and choose the tools you need depending on how you plan to experience Colombia.

To begin with, the chapters have been sequenced in a way that starts broad and gradually narrows into specific themes and destinations. This structure allows you to get an overview of Colombia's essence before delving into its cities, landscapes, and culture. The introduction and early chapters provide foundational knowledge, such as why the country is often regarded as South America's hidden gem and essential tips that first-time visitors will find invaluable. These sections establish a contextual framework, giving you the confidence to approach the rest of the guide with a clear understanding of what to expect.

As you move into the chapters dedicated to Colombia's vibrant cities, you'll find in-depth profiles of urban centers like Bogotá, Medellín, and Cartagena. Each city is explored through its unique identity, historical significance, and key attractions. For example, Bogotá's cultural richness is contrasted with Medellín's innovative spirit and Cartagena's colonial charm. These chapters are designed to help you personalize your journey, whether you're drawn to museums, nightlife, historical landmarks, or food tours. Additionally, the inclusion of lesser-known cities like Bucaramanga or Popayán ensures that the guide caters to both mainstream and off-the-beaten-path travelers.

The sections on natural wonders take a slightly different approach, focusing on Colombia's extraordinary biodiversity and geographical diversity. Here, the goal is to immerse you in the natural beauty of places like Tayrona National Park, the Amazon rainforest, and the Cocora Valley. Practical details, such as how to access these locations, the best times to visit, and what to pack, are woven into the narrative to make planning easier. Whether you're interested in hiking, wildlife observation, or simply soaking in breathtaking scenery, these chapters will help you identify the destinations that resonate most with your preferences.

Cultural exploration is another cornerstone of this guide, and the chapters dedicated to history, traditions, and gastronomy delve deeply into Colombia's soul. For history enthusiasts, sections on pre-Colombian civilizations and colonial heritage provide a window into the country's past, while those interested in modern culture can learn about the impact of music, dance, and festivals. The culinary chapter, meanwhile, is a treat for food lovers, offering insights into regional dishes, drinks, and street food that you simply cannot miss. By the time you finish these chapters, you'll not only have a list of must-try experiences but also a deeper appreciation for the cultural forces that shape Colombia.

Adventure seekers will find the guide equally accommodating, with a dedicated chapter on outdoor activities and adventure sports. Whether you're interested in paragliding over the

Chicamocha Canyon or scuba diving in the crystal-clear waters of San Andrés, this section offers detailed descriptions of what to expect, including safety tips and recommendations for reputable operators. These practical elements are designed to help you make the most of Colombia's outdoor offerings while ensuring a safe and enjoyable experience.

One of the most valuable features of this guide is its focus on hidden gems and off-the-beaten-path destinations. While Colombia's major cities and natural attractions are undeniably captivating, it's often the lesser-known places that leave the strongest impressions. The chapter on hidden gems highlights unique locations like Villa de Leyva, Mompox, and Tierradentro, providing a glimpse into aspects of Colombia that many travelers overlook. These sections are particularly useful for those seeking a more intimate and authentic experience, away from the usual tourist crowds.

To make the guide as user-friendly as possible, practical advice is seamlessly integrated throughout the text. For example, you'll find tips on transportation options, from domestic flights and buses to car rentals and taxis. Currency exchange, safety precautions, and language tips are also addressed, equipping you with the knowledge you need to navigate Colombia confidently. While these details are included in the initial chapters, they are also reinforced in relevant sections to ensure you have the information handy when you need it most.

Another key feature of this guide is its attention to sustainability and responsible travel. Colombia's natural and cultural heritage is one of its greatest assets, and preserving it for future generations is a shared responsibility. Throughout the guide, you'll find suggestions for eco-friendly accommodations, community-based tourism initiatives, and ways to minimize your environmental footprint while traveling. By incorporating these practices into your journey, you can contribute to the ongoing efforts to protect Colombia's unique treasures.

To fully utilize this guide, it's helpful to approach it with a sense of curiosity and flexibility. Think of it as a starting point rather than a rigid blueprint. While the information provided is comprehensive, the beauty of travel lies in its unpredictability and the discoveries made along the way. Use the guide to plan your itinerary, but leave room for spontaneous detours, serendipitous encounters, and moments of unplanned wonder. Colombia is a country that rewards those who take the time to explore it deeply, and this guide is here to support you in that endeavor.

For readers who prefer a more interactive approach, consider pairing this guide with additional resources such as maps, apps, and local tour operators. While the guide offers a wealth of information, having supplementary tools can enhance your experience, especially in remote areas where internet access may be limited. Additionally, engaging with locals—whether through guided tours, community projects, or casual conversations—can provide insights and perspectives that no guidebook can replicate.

Ultimately, the effectiveness of this guide depends on how you choose to use it. Whether you're planning a whirlwind tour of Colombia's highlights or a slow, immersive journey through its landscapes and cultures, the chapters have been designed to adapt to your needs. By taking the time to read through the sections that align with your interests and goals, you'll be better equipped to make informed decisions and create a travel experience that is both memorable and meaningful.

This guide is more than just a collection of recommendations; it's a gateway to understanding and appreciating the essence of Colombia. Every detail, from the descriptions of historical landmarks to the practical travel tips, has been included with care and intention. By using this guide as a tool and a companion, you'll be able to navigate the challenges and joys of exploring South America's hidden heart, uncovering the many layers that make Colombia an extraordinary destination.

# Must-Know Facts About Colombia: Geography, Climate, and People

Colombia is a country of extraordinary contrasts, a place where geography, climate, and people come together to create a uniquely vibrant and diverse identity. Located in the northwest corner of South America, it is the only country on the continent to boast both Caribbean and Pacific coastlines, a feature that underscores its geographical significance and cultural richness. With a land area of over 1.1 million square kilometers, Colombia ranks as the fourth-largest country in South America, but its influence extends far beyond its size. Its varied landscapes, from towering Andean peaks to dense Amazonian rainforests, are mirrored in the diversity of its people, who represent a harmonious blend of indigenous, African, and European heritage. These elements combine to make Colombia one of the most dynamic and multifaceted nations in the world.

Colombia's geography is nothing short of breathtaking in its scope and diversity. The Andes Mountains dominate much of the country, splitting into three distinct ranges as they traverse Colombia from south to north. These mountain chains, known as the Cordillera Occidental, Cordillera Central, and Cordillera Oriental, create an intricate topography of valleys, plateaus, and peaks that define much of the nation's character. Bogotá, the capital city, is perched on a high plateau in the Eastern Andes at an altitude of 2,640 meters above sea level, giving it a cool, temperate climate despite its proximity to the equator. The Andes are also home to fertile valleys that support Colombia's renowned coffee-growing industry, an integral part of its economy and cultural identity. Moving further south, the volcanic landscapes of the southern Andes provide a stark contrast to the verdant slopes of the Coffee Triangle.

To the east of the Andes lies the vast expanse of the Llanos, or plains, which stretch toward the Orinoco River basin. This region is characterized by its flat, open landscapes and serves as a critical ecosystem for Colombia's biodiversity. The Llanos are sparsely populated, providing a haven for wildlife such as capybaras, anteaters, and jaguars. The region's wetlands and grasslands flood seasonally, creating a dynamic environment that supports both agriculture and conservation efforts. Travelers venturing into the Llanos often find themselves captivated by the tranquility of its wide horizons and the opportunity to engage with traditional cowboy culture, known locally as "llanero" life.

Further south and stretching across the nation's southeastern frontier lies the Amazon rainforest, one of the most biodiverse regions on the planet. Colombia's portion of the Amazon accounts for nearly 10% of its total land area, offering a starkly different experience from the highlands and coasts. Here, the humid, tropical climate nurtures an astonishing array of flora and fauna, including thousands of species of plants, birds, insects, and mammals. Leticia, the gateway to Colombia's Amazon region, serves as a base for exploring the jungle's wonders, from pink river dolphins to indigenous communities that have thrived in harmony with their surroundings for centuries. The Amazon is not only a natural marvel but also a cultural and spiritual cornerstone for many indigenous tribes, who view the forest as a sacred entity.

Colombia's western border is defined by the Pacific Ocean, a region that remains one of the country's most underexplored treasures. Rugged cliffs, dense mangroves, and untamed rainforests characterize this coastline, which receives some of the highest rainfall levels in the world. The Pacific Coast is a hotspot for biodiversity, particularly marine life, as migrating humpback whales visit these waters between June and November each year. This region is also home to vibrant Afro-Colombian communities whose cultural traditions, music, and cuisine add a unique layer to Colombia's identity. In contrast, the northern Caribbean coastline offers a completely diffcrent experience, with its warm turquoise waters, coral reefs, and white sandy beaches. Iconic destinations like Cartagena, Santa Marta, and the Rosario Islands attract visitors with their blend of natural beauty and historical significance, while the Guajira

Peninsula's arid deserts and indigenous Wayuu culture offer a glimpse into yet another facet of Colombia's diversity.

The contrast between the Pacific and Caribbean coasts is just one example of how Colombia's climate varies dramatically from region to region. Despite its equatorial location, the country's climate is influenced more by altitude than latitude. This phenomenon, known as altitudinal zonation, divides Colombia into distinct climatic zones ranging from hot lowlands (tierra caliente) to cool highlands (tierra templada) and frigid mountain peaks (tierra fría). Each zone supports different ecosystems and agricultural practices, contributing to the country's remarkable biodiversity and cultural variety. For example, while the lowlands are ideal for cultivating tropical fruits like bananas and pineapples, the highlands are better suited for potatoes, corn, and coffee.

Colombia's people are as diverse as its landscapes, reflecting a rich tapestry of cultural influences that have shaped the nation over centuries. The majority of Colombians identify as mestizo, a mix of European and indigenous ancestry, while significant Afro-Colombian and indigenous populations contribute to the country's multicultural identity. Indigenous groups such as the Wayuu, Kogi, and Embera have preserved their languages, traditions, and spiritual practices despite centuries of colonization and modernization. Afro-Colombians, who are concentrated in the Pacific and Caribbean regions, have significantly shaped Colombia's music, dance, and cuisine, infusing the nation's culture with vibrant rhythms and flavors.

Spanish is the official language of Colombia, but more than 60 indigenous languages are spoken throughout the country, underscoring its linguistic diversity. Efforts to preserve these languages are ongoing, with many communities advocating for bilingual education and cultural preservation. Religion also plays a significant role in Colombian society, with Roman Catholicism being the predominant faith. However, indigenous spiritual practices and Afro-Colombian traditions often coexist alongside Catholic beliefs, creating a unique blend of religious expression.

Colombians are renowned for their warmth, hospitality, and resilience. Family is at the heart of Colombian culture, and social gatherings often revolve around shared meals, music, and dance. The country's love for music is evident in genres like cumbia, vallenato, and salsa, which fill the streets during festivals and celebrations. Events such as Barranquilla's Carnival and Medellín's Feria de las Flores highlight the nation's exuberant spirit and the importance of community. Colombians are also deeply proud of their heritage and natural beauty, and this pride is reflected in their efforts to share their country's treasures with visitors.

While Colombia's modern identity is shaped by its rich cultural heritage, it is also a nation that has undergone significant transformation in recent decades. Once marred by conflict and instability, Colombia has emerged as a symbol of resilience and renewal. The country's cities have become hubs of innovation and creativity, with Medellín earning international recognition for its urban development projects and Bogotá establishing itself as a cultural and artistic capital. These advancements, coupled with a growing focus on sustainable tourism and environmental conservation, have positioned Colombia as a leader in showcasing how a nation can honor its past while embracing its future.

Colombia's geographical diversity, climatic variation, and cultural richness are not just points of interest—they are the essence of what makes the country so captivating. Each region, climate, and community contributes to a mosaic that is as complex as it is beautiful. For travelers, understanding these elements provides a deeper appreciation of the country's identity and the countless stories it has to tell. Whether exploring the high-altitude wonders of the Andes, the lush depths of the Amazon, or the sun-soaked beaches of the Caribbean, visitors are bound to encounter a Colombia that defies expectations and leaves a lasting impression.

# A Brief History of Colombia: From Ancient Civilizations to Modern Times

Colombia's history is a sweeping narrative of ancient civilizations, colonial conquest, struggles for independence, and modern transformation. Each chapter in its timeline reveals a layer of complexity and resilience, with echoes of its past still visible in the country's cultural, political, and social fabric. To understand Colombia today, it is essential to delve into its history, beginning with the indigenous civilizations that first inhabited the land long before the arrival of Europeans.

Long before the Spanish set foot in the Americas, Colombia was home to advanced indigenous cultures that left a profound cultural and spiritual legacy. Among these civilizations were the Muisca, Tairona, and Quimbaya, each known for their distinct contributions to art, architecture, and society. The Muisca, who inhabited the highlands of what is now the Bogotá region, were renowned for their sophisticated agricultural practices and intricate political systems. They excelled in metalworking, particularly in gold, creating elaborate artifacts that have since been unearthed in archaeological sites and museums. The legend of El Dorado, which captivated Spanish conquistadors and European explorers, originated from Muisca rituals, where gold dust was scattered into sacred lakes during ceremonies.

Meanwhile, the Tairona people thrived in the Sierra Nevada de Santa Marta, building complex urban centers with stone terraces, roads, and aqueducts that harmonized with the mountainous terrain. Their remarkable skills in engineering and their spiritual connection to nature remain evident in the ruins of Ciudad Perdida, or the "Lost City," a site that predates Peru's Machu Picchu by several centuries. The Quimbaya civilization, located in the central regions of the country, is celebrated for its unparalleled goldsmithing techniques, producing artifacts that remain some of the most exquisite examples of pre-Colombian art. These civilizations, though diverse in culture and geography, shared a profound respect for the land, a value that persists among many indigenous communities in Colombia today.

The arrival of the Spanish in 1499 marked the beginning of a transformative and often devastating period in Colombia's history. Spanish explorers, led by Alonso de Ojeda, were drawn to the region by tales of wealth and abundance, particularly the fabled El Dorado. The initial contact with indigenous populations set the stage for conquest, as Spanish forces sought to claim territory and resources for the Spanish Crown. In 1538, Gonzalo Jiménez de Quesada founded the city of Santa Fe de Bogotá, establishing it as the capital of the New Kingdom of Granada, a colonial territory that encompassed much of present-day Colombia, Venezuela, Ecuador, and Panama.

The colonial period brought profound changes to the region, as indigenous populations were decimated by disease, forced labor, and violent subjugation. The encomienda system, a feudal-like arrangement, allowed Spanish colonists to extract labor and tribute from indigenous communities, further eroding their way of life. At the same time, African slaves were brought to Colombia to work in mines, plantations, and households, adding another layer to the country's complex cultural mosaic. Despite these hardships, indigenous and African communities resisted oppression in various forms, from armed uprisings to the preservation of cultural traditions that have endured to this day.

The colonial era also saw the construction of cities, churches, and infrastructure that would shape Colombia's urban landscape. Cartagena, established as a key port city, became a hub for trade and a target for pirates, necessitating the construction of massive fortifications like the Castillo San Felipe de Barajas. These architectural feats stand as enduring symbols of Colombia's colonial past, even as they remind us of the exploitation and conflict that defined the era.

The late 18th and early 19th centuries marked a turning point in Colombia's history, as the winds of independence swept across Latin America. Inspired by Enlightenment ideals and the success of revolutions in the United States and France, local leaders began to challenge Spanish rule. The struggle for independence gained momentum in 1810, when a political uprising in Bogotá led to the establishment of a provisional government. However, the path to independence was far from straightforward, as Spanish forces sought to regain control, resulting in years of conflict and instability.

One of the most pivotal figures in Colombia's fight for independence was Simón Bolívar, a military and political leader who envisioned a united South America free from colonial rule. Bolívar's campaigns against Spanish forces culminated in the decisive Battle of Boyacá on August 7, 1819, a victory that secured the independence of the New Kingdom of Granada. Shortly thereafter, the Republic of Colombia was established, encompassing modern-day Colombia, Venezuela, Ecuador, and Panama. However, Bolívar's dream of a united Gran Colombia was short-lived, as political and regional divisions led to the dissolution of the republic in 1831.

The post-independence period was marked by political turbulence, as Colombia grappled with the challenges of nation-building. The 19th century saw a series of civil wars, power struggles, and ideological conflicts between conservatives and liberals, each vying for control of the country's future. These divisions were not merely political but also reflected deeper tensions over issues such as land ownership, church-state relations, and regional autonomy. The Thousand Days' War (1899–1902), a brutal conflict between liberals and conservatives, devastated the country and set the stage for further instability in the 20th century.

The loss of Panama in 1903 was a significant blow to Colombia's territorial integrity and national psyche. After years of U.S. intervention and local unrest, Panama declared independence from Colombia, facilitated by the United States' interest in constructing the Panama Canal. This event underscored Colombia's vulnerability to external influences and highlighted the geopolitical realities of the region.

The 20th century brought new challenges and opportunities for Colombia as it sought to modernize and industrialize. The rise of the coffee industry transformed the country's economy, making it one of the world's leading coffee exporters. However, economic growth was accompanied by social inequality and rural unrest, as landless peasants and marginalized communities demanded reforms. These tensions would later give rise to guerrilla movements, most notably the Revolutionary Armed Forces of Colombia (FARC), which emerged in the 1960s as a Marxist-Leninist insurgency.

The latter half of the 20th century was defined by the dual challenges of guerrilla warfare and the rise of drug cartels. Colombia became a major player in the global drug trade, with cartels like Medellín and Cali amassing immense power and wealth. The violence and corruption associated with the drug trade plunged the country into a state of crisis, as government forces, paramilitary groups, and guerrilla factions vied for control. High-profile assassinations, kidnappings, and bombings became grim hallmarks of this period, tarnishing Colombia's international reputation.

Despite these dark chapters, Colombia's resilience and determination have driven its transformation in recent decades. The turn of the 21st century saw significant efforts to address internal conflicts, with the Colombian government implementing security reforms and pursuing peace negotiations. The 2016 peace agreement with the FARC marked a historic milestone, though challenges remain in achieving lasting peace and addressing the root causes of conflict.

Today, Colombia stands as a testament to the power of renewal and reinvention. Its cities have become hubs of innovation, culture, and tourism, while its people continue to celebrate their heritage with pride. The country's history, though marked by struggle, is also a story of resilience, creativity, and hope. By understanding Colombia's past, visitors can gain a deeper appreciation for the complexities and beauty of this remarkable nation.

# CHAPTER 1: COLOMBIA'S VIBRANT CITIES

## Bogotá: The Capital's Cultural and Historical Treasures

Bogotá, Colombia's sprawling capital, is a city of contrasts where history and modernity collide against a backdrop of the Andes mountains. At an altitude of 2,640 meters (8,660 feet) above sea level, it is one of the highest capitals in the world, and its unique location influences everything from its climate to its culture. Home to over eight million people, Bogotá is a vibrant mosaic of neighborhoods, each with its own distinct personality. The city pulses with energy, creativity, and a deep sense of history, offering visitors an unparalleled opportunity to explore Colombia's cultural and historical roots while experiencing its contemporary dynamism.

The beating heart of Bogotá's historical identity is La Candelaria, the city's oldest neighborhood and a living museum of colonial architecture, cobbled streets, and colorful facades. Walking through its narrow lanes feels like stepping back in time, as colonial-era buildings house everything from small cafes and artisan shops to libraries and government offices. The neighborhood is home to some of Bogotá's most iconic landmarks, including Plaza de Bolívar, the city's main square. This expansive plaza is surrounded by historic buildings such as the neoclassical Capitolio Nacional, the seat of Colombia's Congress, and the Catedral Primada de Colombia, an imposing cathedral that dominates the square. This area has been the political and cultural center of Bogotá since its founding in 1538, and its significance is palpable in every corner.

La Candelaria is also a hub for Bogotá's thriving artistic scene. The neighborhood's walls are adorned with vibrant murals and graffiti, turning the streets into an open-air gallery. Bogotá has embraced street art as a legitimate form of artistic expression, and La Candelaria is one of the best places to witness this creativity firsthand. Many murals tell stories of Colombia's history, struggles, and resilience, blending political commentary with striking visual imagery. Guided street art tours are popular here, offering insights into the artists' techniques and the social messages behind their work. Art and history converge in La Candelaria, creating an atmosphere that is both captivating and thought-provoking.

For those seeking to immerse themselves in Bogotá's rich cultural heritage, the city's museums provide a treasure trove of knowledge and artifacts. The Gold Museum (Museo del Oro) is perhaps the most famous, housing one of the largest collections of pre-Columbian gold artifacts in the world. Its exhibits showcase the extraordinary craftsmanship of indigenous cultures like the Muisca, whose goldwork inspired the legend of El Dorado. Each piece tells a story, not only of the societies that created them but also of the spiritual and symbolic significance that gold held in their lives. A visit to the Gold Museum offers a deeper understanding of Colombia's ancient civilizations and their enduring impact on the country's identity.

Another must-visit institution is the Botero Museum, which celebrates the work of Fernando Botero, Colombia's most renowned artist. Known for his distinctive style of exaggerated proportions, Botero's paintings and sculptures are instantly recognizable and often infused with humor and irony. The museum, housed in a beautifully restored colonial mansion, also features works by international masters such as Picasso, Monet, and Dalí, making it a cultural gem that bridges Colombian and global art. Admission to the Botero Museum is free, underscoring Bogotá's commitment to making art accessible to all.

Beyond its museums and galleries, Bogotá's cultural landscape is enriched by its theaters, music venues, and festivals. The city is a hub for the performing arts, with institutions like the Teatro Colón offering world-class productions of opera, ballet, and theater. The Teatro Mayor Julio Mario Santo Domingo hosts a diverse array of performances, from classical music to contemporary dance. Bogotá's music scene reflects the country's diversity, encompassing genres like cumbia, vallenato, salsa, and rock. The city's nightlife districts, such as Zona Rosa and Chapinero, come alive with live music venues and clubs where locals and visitors dance the night away.

Bogotá's connection to its history is not confined to its cultural institutions; it is also evident in its public spaces and monuments. Monserrate, a mountain that rises sharply above the city, is both a natural landmark and a spiritual site. Accessible by cable car, funicular, or a challenging hike, Monserrate offers breathtaking panoramic views of Bogotá and the surrounding valley. At its summit stands a whitewashed church, a pilgrimage site for devout Colombians and a place of reflection for visitors of all backgrounds. The journey to Monserrate is as much about the experience as the destination, providing a sense of Bogotá's spiritual and geographic grandeur.

Parque Simón Bolívar, Bogotá's largest urban park, serves as a green oasis in the midst of the bustling city. Named after the liberator of much of South America, the park is a place where history and leisure intersect. Its expansive grounds include a lake, walking trails, and open spaces for concerts and cultural events. The park is a testament to Bogotá's efforts to balance urban development with environmental stewardship, offering residents and tourists a space to relax, exercise, and connect with nature.

The city's modernity is perhaps most evident in neighborhoods like Chapinero and Zona G, where Bogotá's culinary and entrepreneurial spirit shines. Zona G, short for "Gourmet Zone," is a food lover's paradise, offering a diverse range of dining experiences that highlight both traditional Colombian flavors and international cuisines. From hearty ajiaco soup to innovative fusion dishes, Bogotá's culinary scene reflects the city's cosmopolitan character and its deep-rooted gastronomic traditions. Chapinero, meanwhile, is a vibrant district known for its eclectic mix of shops, cafes, and nightlife. Its bohemian atmosphere attracts artists, students, and entrepreneurs, making it one of Bogotá's most dynamic areas.

Transportation in Bogotá can be an adventure in itself, as the city's size and elevation create unique challenges. The TransMilenio, a bus rapid transit system, serves as the backbone of Bogotá's public transportation network, offering an efficient way to navigate the city despite its often-crowded conditions. Cycling is another popular option, thanks to Bogotá's extensive network of bike lanes and its celebrated Ciclovía event, during which major streets are closed to motor vehicles on Sundays to allow cyclists, joggers, and pedestrians to take over. These initiatives reflect Bogotá's commitment to sustainability and innovation in urban planning.

Despite its many attractions, Bogotá can be overwhelming for first-time visitors. Its sheer scale and altitude require some adjustment, but the rewards of exploring the city far outweigh the challenges. Interacting with its people, who are known for their warmth and hospitality, often provides some of the most memorable moments of any visit. Whether engaging in a conversation with a street vendor, joining locals for a game of tejo (a traditional Colombian sport), or simply observing daily life in a bustling plaza, Bogotá invites visitors to connect on a personal level.

The city's resilience and adaptability are evident in its ability to honor its past while embracing change. From its colonial roots in La Candelaria to its modern skyline and innovative public spaces, Bogotá is a city that defies easy categorization. It is a place where history is alive, where art and culture flourish, and where the pulse of modern Colombia can be felt most vividly. For those willing to explore its many layers, Bogotá offers an experience that is as enriching as it is unforgettable.

# Medellín: The City of Eternal Spring

Medellín, Colombia's second-largest city, is often referred to as the "City of Eternal Spring," a name earned for its year-round temperate climate and the warmth it exudes—not just in weather, but in spirit. Nestled in the Aburrá Valley, surrounded by lush green mountains that rise like sentinels, Medellín has undergone a remarkable transformation over the past few decades. Once infamous for its association with violence and the drug trade, the city has reinvented itself into a vibrant hub of innovation, culture, and social progress. For travelers, Medellín offers a unique blend of urban sophistication and natural beauty, where every corner reveals a story of resilience, community, and creativity.

The city's geography plays an integral role in shaping its character. Located at an altitude of approximately 1,500 meters (4,920 feet) above sea level, Medellín enjoys a climate that hovers between 18 and 24 degrees Celsius (64 to 75 degrees Fahrenheit) throughout the year. This pleasant weather fosters an outdoor lifestyle, and it's not uncommon to see locals, known as "Paisas," gathering in parks, plazas, and open-air cafes. The surrounding mountains not only frame the city with stunning vistas but also serve as a constant reminder of Medellín's connection to nature. The valley's steep slopes are dotted with neighborhoods that climb the hillsides, creating a dramatic urban landscape that is as dynamic as it is picturesque.

Medellín's transformation is perhaps best illustrated by its public transportation system, which serves as both a practical utility and a symbol of social change. The city's metro system is the pride of Medellín, not only for its efficiency and cleanliness but also for its role in connecting disparate communities. Complementing the metro are the Metrocable lines, a series of cable cars that reach the hillside neighborhoods once isolated by geography and poverty. These cable cars have become an emblem of inclusion, bridging physical and social divides while offering passengers breathtaking views of the city below. For visitors, riding the Metrocable isn't just a way to get from one point to another—it's an opportunity to witness Medellín's innovative approach to urban development firsthand.

At the heart of Medellín's cultural scene is the city center, a bustling area where old and new converge. Plaza Botero, named for the celebrated Colombian artist Fernando Botero, is a must-visit destination. The plaza is home to 23 of Botero's larger-than-life bronze sculptures, each imbued with his signature style of exaggerated proportions. Surrounding the plaza are landmarks like the Museo de Antioquia, which houses an impressive collection of Botero's works alongside exhibits that explore the region's history and culture. The nearby Rafael Uribe Uribe Palace of Culture, with its striking Gothic Revival architecture, adds another layer of intrigue to the area.

Medellín's neighborhoods, each with its distinct identity, offer a window into the city's soul. El Poblado, often referred to as the city's upscale district, is a favorite among travelers for its trendy restaurants, boutique hotels, and lively nightlife. Parque Lleras, located in the heart of El Poblado, serves as a social hub where locals and visitors mingle over cocktails and music. In contrast, Laureles exudes a more laid-back atmosphere, with tree-lined streets, family-owned eateries, and a strong sense of community. For those seeking an authentic taste of Medellín, the Comuna 13 neighborhood provides a powerful narrative of transformation. Once known as one of the most dangerous areas in the city, Comuna 13 has become a symbol of hope and resilience. Its colorful murals, vibrant street art, and outdoor escalators tell a story of a community that refused to be defined by its past.

The people of Medellín, the Paisas, are renowned for their hospitality and entrepreneurial spirit. Their warmth and pride in their city are palpable, and interactions with locals often leave a lasting impression on visitors. Whether it's a taxi driver sharing his thoughts on Medellín's progress or a vendor offering a taste of freshly cut mango, these moments of connection add depth to the experience of exploring the city. Paisas are also known for their strong work ethic and ingenuity, qualities that have driven Medellín's reputation as an innovation hub. The city has been recognized globally for its urban planning initiatives, technological advancements, and commitment to social equity, earning it the title of "Innovative City of the Year" in 2013.

Medellín's festivals are a testament to its vibrant culture and love for celebration. The Feria de las Flores, or Festival of Flowers, held annually in August, is the city's most iconic event. What began as a modest flower parade in the 1950s has evolved into a week-long extravaganza featuring concerts, horse parades, and the famed Silleteros Parade, in which flower farmers carry elaborate floral arrangements on their backs. The festival is a joyful expression of Medellín's agricultural heritage and a celebration of life and beauty. Another notable event is the Medellín Tango Festival, a nod to the city's historical connection to the Argentine dance. The festival attracts tango enthusiasts from around the world, showcasing Medellín's role as a cultural crossroads.

For nature lovers, Medellín serves as a gateway to the surrounding region, where outdoor adventures abound. Just a short drive from the city lies Arví Park, an ecological reserve that offers a serene escape from urban life. The park, accessible via a Metrocable ride followed by a scenic gondola journey, features hiking trails, picnic areas, and opportunities for birdwatching. Further afield, the colorful town of Guatapé and the towering Rock of El Peñol provide a perfect day trip destination. Climbing the 740 steps to the top of El Peñol rewards visitors with panoramic views of a sprawling reservoir dotted with emerald-green islands.

Medellín's culinary scene reflects the city's dynamic character, blending traditional flavors with modern innovation. The Bandeja Paisa, a hearty platter featuring beans, rice, chorizo, ground beef, fried egg, and avocado, is a quintessential dish that embodies the region's culinary heritage. Street food, from arepas filled with cheese to buñuelos and empanadas, offers a taste of Medellín's everyday flavors. Meanwhile, the city's burgeoning restaurant scene showcases the creativity of local chefs who are redefining Colombian cuisine. Dining in Medellín is not just about sustenance—it's an opportunity to explore the city's identity through its food.

The resilience of Medellín's people and their commitment to progress stand as a testament to the city's remarkable journey. While its past is marked by challenges, Medellín has emerged as a beacon of hope and innovation, a city that has embraced change while staying true to its roots. For visitors, Medellín offers more than just sights and attractions—it offers an invitation to witness a vibrant community that has turned adversity into opportunity. Every street, every mural, and every handshake tells a story of a city that refuses to be defined by its past but instead chooses to shape its future.

## Cartagena: A Caribbean Jewel Steeped in History

Cartagena, perched on Colombia's Caribbean coast, is a city that seems to shimmer in golden hues, its colonial-era walls and sunlit beaches creating a striking blend of history and tropical allure. Known officially as Cartagena de Indias, this enchanting destination is a living museum of Colombia's colonial past, while simultaneously embracing its vibrant, modern identity. Walking its cobblestone streets, with colorful balconies overflowing with bougainvillea and the echoes of horse-drawn carriages, feels like stepping into another era. Yet Cartagena is more than its romantic veneer. Beneath its picturesque surface lies a city deeply shaped by its strategic importance, its role in the transatlantic world, and its enduring cultural vibrancy.

The city's history begins in 1533 when Pedro de Heredia founded Cartagena as a Spanish settlement. Its location, with a protected harbor and easy access to trade routes, made it one of the most important ports in the Spanish Empire. Gold, silver, and other treasures from the New World passed through Cartagena on their way to Europe, making the city not only a hub of wealth but also a target for pirates and privateers. The likes of Francis Drake and other infamous figures laid siege to Cartagena, plundering its riches and leaving their mark on the city's collective memory. As a response to these repeated attacks, the Spanish Crown invested heavily in fortifying the city, constructing an elaborate system of walls and bastions that still stand today.

At the heart of Cartagena's historic identity is its walled city, or Ciudad Amurallada. Encircled by thick stone walls that stretch nearly seven miles, this UNESCO World Heritage Site is a masterpiece of colonial architecture and urban planning. Walking along the walls offers breathtaking views of both the Caribbean Sea and the city's patchwork of colorful rooftops. Within these walls lies a labyrinth of narrow streets, plazas, and churches that have been meticulously preserved. The Plaza de los Coches, once a marketplace for enslaved people during the colonial era, now bustles with vendors selling sweets and crafts, its dark history a poignant contrast to its lively present.

The Castillo San Felipe de Barajas is another testament to Cartagena's strategic and military significance. This imposing fortress, perched on San Lázaro Hill, is considered one of the greatest feats of Spanish military engineering in the Americas. Built to protect the city from land and sea attacks, the fortress features a network of tunnels designed for communication and escape during sieges. Exploring its labyrinthine passageways gives visitors a sense of the ingenuity and resourcefulness required to defend Cartagena's wealth. From the top of the fortress, panoramic views of the city and the harbor serve as a reminder of why this location was so fiercely contested.

Cartagena's history is also inextricably linked to the transatlantic slave trade. As one of the main ports for enslaved Africans brought to the Americas, the city became a cultural melting pot, blending African, indigenous, and European influences. This legacy is evident in Cartagena's music, cuisine, and traditions, which are infused with the rhythms and flavors of Africa. The San Pedro Claver Church and its adjacent museum offer a window into this chapter of Cartagena's past. Named after Saint Peter Claver, a Jesuit priest who dedicated his life to ministering to enslaved Africans, the church stands as a symbol of both the suffering and resilience of those who passed through its port.

Beyond its historical significance, Cartagena is a celebration of life and culture. The city's vibrant streets are alive with music, from traditional cumbia and champeta rhythms to the melodies of street performers strumming guitars or playing drums. The Getsemaní neighborhood, once a working-class district, has emerged as a hub of creativity and nightlife. Its walls are adorned with colorful murals that tell stories of resistance, identity, and community. In the evenings, Plaza Trinidad becomes a gathering place for locals and visitors alike, with impromptu dance performances, food vendors, and a palpable sense of joy that's impossible to resist.

Cartagena's culinary scene is a sensory journey that reflects its diverse heritage and coastal bounty. The city's markets, such as Mercado de Bazurto, are a chaotic yet fascinating introduction to local flavors. Here, you'll find tropical fruits like lulo and guanábana, freshly caught seafood, and spices that define the region's cuisine. Must-try dishes include cazuela de mariscos, a rich seafood stew made with coconut milk, and arepas de huevo, a fried corn cake stuffed with egg and meat. Street food, from skewered meats to fresh mango slices sprinkled with lime and salt, offers an authentic taste of Cartagena's daily life. Dining at one of the city's upscale restaurants, many of which are housed in beautifully restored colonial buildings, provides a modern twist on traditional flavors, showcasing the creativity of Cartagena's chefs.

The city's Caribbean location also means that its beaches play an essential role in its identity. While the beaches near the urban area, such as Bocagrande, are popular for their convenience, the true gems lie just offshore. The Rosario Islands, an archipelago of coral reefs and turquoise waters, offer a tranquil escape from the bustling city. Accessible by boat, these islands are perfect for snorkeling, diving, or simply relaxing on pristine beaches. Playa Blanca, located on the Barú Peninsula, is another favorite destination, known for its powdery white sand and crystal-clear waters. These coastal retreats complement Cartagena's urban charms, providing a balance between history and relaxation.

Cartagena is also a city of festivals, where its residents' love for celebration is on full display. The Hay Festival, an international literary event held each January, attracts writers, thinkers, and artists from around the world. The Cartagena International Music Festival, celebrated in the city's historic venues, showcases a wide range of classical and contemporary music. But perhaps the most distinctly Colombian event is the November Independence Celebrations, a lively and colorful commemoration of Cartagena's role as the first city in Colombia to declare independence from Spanish rule. Parades, concerts, and beauty pageants fill the streets, embodying the city's spirit of pride and resilience.

What sets Cartagena apart is its ability to weave past and present into a seamless tapestry. Its history is not confined to museums or monuments but lives on in its traditions, its people, and its streets. The city's resilience, evident in its ability to overcome centuries of conflict and colonization, mirrors the resilience of Colombia itself. Yet Cartagena is not content to remain in the past. Its embrace of tourism, art, and gastronomy positions it as a forward-thinking city that welcomes the world while staying true to its roots.

For those who visit Cartagena, the city offers more than just a picturesque backdrop. It is an invitation to explore a place where every corner tells a story, where the past and present coexist in vivid harmony. Whether you're wandering through the walled city, savoring a plate of fresh seafood by the sea, or dancing to the rhythms of the Caribbean night, Cartagena leaves an indelible impression. It is a city that captures the soul of Colombia, a place where history is not just remembered but celebrated, and where every moment feels steeped in magic.

## Cali: Salsa, Nightlife, and Afro-Colombian Culture

Cali, the vibrant heart of Colombia's Valle del Cauca region, pulses with a rhythm unlike any other city in the country. Known as the world's salsa capital, Cali is a place where life unfolds to the beat of drums, the strum of guitars, and the sway of hips. Yet there is so much more to this city than its famous nightlife. Beneath the music lies a rich tapestry of

Afro-Colombian heritage, cultural pride, and dynamic urban energy. Cali is a city where tradition and modernity meet, where the heat of the day gives way to electric nights, and where the essence of Colombia's diverse identity comes alive in every corner.

The city's identity is inseparable from its music, with salsa as its lifeblood. While salsa originated in the Caribbean, Cali has claimed the genre as its own, shaping it into a cultural phenomenon that permeates every aspect of life here. It's not just music—it's a way of being. From the moment you step into the city, the sounds of salsa surround you, spilling out from local radio stations, bustling markets, and open dance studios. For the uninitiated, the passion for this genre might seem overwhelming, but in Cali, salsa is an open invitation. Dance schools, ranging from professional academies to informal neighborhood gatherings, welcome anyone willing to learn, no matter their skill level. Even if you've never danced a step in your life, the city's infectious energy will have you moving.

The salsa clubs of Cali are legendary, each with its own personality and history. Places like Zaperoco and La Topa Tolondra are more than just nightspots; they are cultural institutions where locals and visitors come together to celebrate life. Inside, the air hums with excitement, as dancers glide across the floor with a combination of practiced precision and raw emotion. The atmosphere is electric, with live bands often taking center stage, their brass sections and percussionists driving the crowd into a frenzy. The connection between the music, the dancers, and the audience is almost palpable—it's not just entertainment; it's a communion. Even for those who prefer to sit and watch, the experience is unforgettable, offering a window into Cali's soul.

Beyond its nightlife, Cali is a city deeply rooted in Afro-Colombian culture, a legacy of its history as a hub for African-descended communities. This influence is most visible in the neighborhoods of the city's eastern and southern districts, such as Aguablanca, where Afro-Colombian traditions are preserved and celebrated. The annual Petronio Álvarez

Festival, named after the legendary composer, is the pinnacle of Afro-Colombian cultural expression in Cali. This week-long event brings together musicians, dancers, and artisans from across the Pacific Coast to showcase the rich heritage of the region. The festival is a sensory overload of traditional marimba rhythms, vibrant costumes, and delicious cuisine, all set against the backdrop of Cali's undeniable energy.

Afro-Colombian food in Cali is a reflection of the region's cultural melting pot. Dishes like sancocho de pescado, a hearty fish stew flavored with coconut milk and herbs, speak to the Pacific Coast's culinary traditions. Street food, such as aborrajados (fried plantains stuffed with cheese) and chontaduro (palm fruits served with honey or salt), offers a taste of everyday life in Cali. Visiting local markets like Galería Alameda provides an even deeper connection to the city's food culture. Here, vendors sell everything from fresh tropical fruits to homemade tamales, their stalls bursting with color and aroma. Strolling through the market is an immersive experience, where every bite tells a story of the city's Afro-Colombian and indigenous heritage.

Cali's relationship with its Afro-Colombian identity extends beyond music and food; it's also expressed through art and storytelling. The city's murals and street art are vibrant testaments to its cultural richness, depicting scenes of resilience, joy, and history. Many of these works can be found in the neighborhood of San Antonio, a bohemian district known for its colonial architecture and creative spirit. The area's narrow streets and hillside views make it a favorite spot for both locals and tourists, offering a quieter but no less vibrant side of Cali. At night, the neighborhood transforms, as musicians and storytellers gather in its plazas, their performances echoing the rhythms of the city's past and present.

Cali's location in the fertile Cauca Valley has also shaped its identity, making it one of Colombia's agricultural powerhouses. Sugarcane fields stretch for miles around the city, their harvest feeding into a thriving sugar industry that has long been central to the region's economy. The sprawling haciendas that dot the valley are remnants of this history, some of which have been converted into museums and cultural sites. These estates offer a glimpse into the region's colonial past while serving as reminders of the social and economic transformations that have defined Cali over the centuries. Visiting one of these haciendas provides a deeper understanding of how the land and its people have shaped each other.

Modern Cali is a city of contrasts, where bustling urban life meets the tranquility of its natural surroundings. The Río Cali, which winds through the heart of the city, serves as a gathering place for locals, particularly along its revitalized riverwalk. Parks like Cerro de las Tres Cruces and Cristo Rey offer not only panoramic views of the city but also spaces for recreation and reflection. On weekends, these spots come alive with families, hikers, and fitness enthusiasts, all drawn by the city's outdoor lifestyle. The nearby Farallones de Cali National Park, with its rugged mountain terrain and diverse ecosystems, offers an escape for those seeking adventure or a deeper connection with nature.

Cali's embrace of its Afro-Colombian roots and its devotion to salsa are complemented by a spirit of resilience and progress. The city has faced challenges, from social inequality to periods of violence, but its people have continually found ways to rise above. This spirit is perhaps best embodied in its younger generations, who are redefining Cali's future through entrepreneurship, art, and activism. Initiatives like community dance programs and urban farming projects are transforming neighborhoods and providing opportunities for those who need them most. These efforts reflect a city that is not only proud of its past but also committed to building a better future.

For visitors, Cali is an experience that stays with you long after you've left. It's the sound of a salsa band warming up in a dimly lit club, the taste of a fresh mango sprinkled with lime, the sight of a mural that tells a story of resilience, and the feeling of being swept up in the city's unrelenting energy. Cali doesn't just invite you to visit—it challenges you to engage, to move, to feel. It's a place where life is lived with passion, where every moment is an opportunity to celebrate, and where the heartbeat of Colombia can be felt most strongly. To come to Cali is to experience a city that dances through life, never missing a beat.

## Barranquilla: Carnival and Coastal Charm

Barranquilla, a bustling port city on Colombia's Caribbean coast, is a place where vibrant culture, rich traditions, and coastal charm converge. Known as the "Golden Gate of Colombia" for its historic role as a hub of trade and immigration, Barranquilla has grown into a dynamic city that embodies the spirit of the Caribbean. Its streets hum with the energy of a city that celebrates life, and nowhere is this more evident than during its world-famous Carnival, a dazzling spectacle of music, dance, and pageantry that rivals some of the greatest festivals in the world. Yet, beyond the Carnival and its festive exuberance, Barranquilla offers a wealth of experiences that reflect its unique coastal identity and its role as a melting pot of cultures.

The history of Barranquilla is deeply intertwined with its location along the Magdalena River and its proximity to the Caribbean Sea. These waterways have long served as lifelines for trade, connecting the city to the interior of Colombia as well as to global markets. During the late 19th and early 20th centuries, Barranquilla became a key entry point for European immigrants, particularly from the Middle East, Germany, and Italy. This influx of people brought with it diverse cultural influences that continue to shape the city's identity today. The blend of indigenous, African, European, and Middle Eastern traditions is evident in everything from Barranquilla's cuisine to its architecture, making it one of Colombia's most culturally diverse cities.

The highlight of Barranquilla's cultural calendar is undoubtedly its Carnival, a UNESCO-recognized event that transforms the city into a kaleidoscope of color and rhythm.

Held in the days leading up to Ash Wednesday, Carnival is a four-day explosion of joy, creativity, and tradition. The festival's roots can be traced back to colonial times, when European religious celebrations merged with African and indigenous rituals to create a uniquely Caribbean expression of identity. Today, Carnival is a celebration of Barranquilla's cultural heritage, bringing together thousands of performers, musicians, and dancers in an event that captivates both locals and visitors.

The heart of Carnival lies in its parades, each of which showcases a different aspect of Barranquilla's cultural tapestry. The Battle of the Flowers, the festival's most iconic event, features elaborately decorated floats, costumed dancers, and traditional music that fills the air with an infectious energy. Performers dressed as marimondas, with their colorful masks and playful antics, embody the spirit of satire and irreverence that is central to the Carnival's ethos. Meanwhile, the Great Parade highlights folkloric dances such as cumbia, mapalé, and garabato, each with its own distinct rhythms and movements that tell stories of the region's history and traditions. The music of Carnival, driven by the beats of drums, brass instruments, and the accordion strains of vallenato, underscores the festival's dynamic energy.

For those who want to immerse themselves in the spirit of Carnival beyond the parades, the city's streets and plazas come alive with parties, concerts, and cultural events. The Carnival Queen and King Momo, figures who preside over the festivities, lead the celebrations with charisma and flair. The events are not confined to large venues; they spill into neighborhoods and public spaces, where locals gather to dance, eat, and enjoy the festive atmosphere. Even for those who visit Barranquilla outside of Carnival season, the city's Carnival Museum offers a glimpse into the history and traditions of this extraordinary event. The museum showcases costumes, masks, and archival footage, providing insight into the artistry and cultural significance of Carnival.

Beyond the Carnival, Barranquilla's coastal identity is reflected in its culinary traditions, which draw heavily on the bounty of the sea. Seafood dishes such as cazuela de mariscos, a rich seafood stew, and fried fish served with coconut rice and patacones (fried plantains) are staples of the local diet. The city's street food scene is equally vibrant, offering delights like arepas de huevo (corn cakes stuffed with egg) and carimañolas (fried yucca rolls filled with meat or cheese). Markets such as Mercado de Barranquillita provide a sensory journey through the region's flavors, with stalls overflowing with tropical fruits, fresh fish, and aromatic spices. Dining in Barranquilla is more than just a meal—it's an experience that connects visitors to the city's Caribbean roots.

The city's cultural richness extends to its architecture and public spaces, which reflect its historical and modern identities. The neighborhood of El Prado, developed in the early 20th century, is a showcase of elegant mansions and tree-lined streets that speak to Barranquilla's cosmopolitan past. These homes, many of which feature Art Deco and neoclassical designs, stand as a testament to the city's history as a hub of wealth and influence. In contrast, the more modern areas of the city, such as the Paseo Bolívar and the Gran Malecón along the Magdalena River, highlight Barranquilla's forward-looking spirit. The Gran Malecón, in particular, has become a favorite spot for both locals and tourists, offering scenic views, recreational areas, and a lively atmosphere that captures the essence of the city.

Barranquilla's connection to the arts is another facet of its cultural identity. The city has produced some of Colombia's most celebrated artists, writers, and musicians, including the internationally renowned singer Shakira. Art galleries and cultural institutions, such as the Museo del Caribe, provide a deeper understanding of the region's history and artistic traditions. The museum's exhibits explore themes ranging from the indigenous cultures of the Caribbean coast to the impact of immigration on Barranquilla's identity. For fans of literature, the city's ties to Gabriel García Márquez, who spent part of his early career in Barranquilla, add another layer of cultural significance.

The natural beauty of Barranquilla's surroundings also contributes to its appeal. While the city itself is not known for its beaches, its location along the Caribbean coast makes it a gateway to nearby coastal destinations. Just a short drive away, visitors can find pristine beaches such as Puerto Colombia and Pradomar, where the warm waters and golden sands provide a tranquil escape from the bustling city. The mangroves and wetlands of the Ciénaga de Mallorquín, located on the city's outskirts, offer opportunities for birdwatching and ecotourism, showcasing the region's ecological diversity.

What sets Barranquilla apart is its ability to balance its rich cultural heritage with a dynamic, modern energy. The city's residents, known as Barranquilleros, are proud of their traditions but also embrace progress and innovation. This duality is evident in the city's festivals, food, architecture, and arts, all of which reflect a deep connection to the past while looking toward the future. Barranquilla is not just a place to visit—it's a city to experience, where every moment feels infused with the warmth and vibrancy of the Caribbean. Whether you're dancing in the streets during Carnival, savoring a plate of fresh seafood by the river, or exploring the stories of its diverse communities, Barranquilla offers an unforgettable glimpse into the heart of Colombia's coastal culture.

## Santa Marta: Gateway to Tayrona National Park

Santa Marta, Colombia's oldest surviving city and a bustling port along the Caribbean coast, is a place where history, nature, and culture come together in perfect harmony. Founded in 1525 by Spanish conquistador Rodrigo de Bastidas, it holds the distinction of being the first Spanish settlement in Colombia. Yet, despite its historical significance, Santa Marta is far from being a relic of the past. Today, it serves as a vibrant gateway to some of Colombia's most breathtaking natural attractions, particularly Tayrona National Park. The city's tropical charm, coupled with its proximity to the Sierra Nevada de Santa Marta mountains and the turquoise waters of the Caribbean, creates a destination that is as multifaceted as it is unforgettable.

The historic center of Santa Marta is the beating heart of the city, a maze of narrow streets lined with colonial-era buildings that have been beautifully preserved or restored. Here, visitors can wander through plazas shaded by palm trees, where locals gather to socialize, and street vendors sell everything from fresh coconuts to handmade crafts. The centerpiece of the historic district is the Santa Marta Cathedral, a whitewashed structure with a simple elegance that belies its historical significance. As one of the oldest cathedrals in South America, it is said to be the final resting place of Rodrigo de Bastidas, the city's founder. Its cool, quiet interior provides a welcome respite from the tropical heat, and its historical gravitas adds depth to any visit.

Nearby, the Quinta de San Pedro Alejandrino offers another glimpse into Santa Marta's historical legacy. This sprawling hacienda, surrounded by lush gardens, was the final home of Simón Bolívar, the liberator of much of South America. Bolívar spent his last days here in 1830, and the property has since been transformed into a museum dedicated to his life and achievements. Wandering through its corridors and grounds, visitors can almost feel the weight of history, as artifacts, documents, and Bolívar's personal belongings paint a vivid picture of his final moments. The Quinta is more than just a museum; it is a place of reverence, a reminder of the sacrifices made in the quest for independence.

While Santa Marta's historic landmarks are undeniably compelling, its natural surroundings are what truly set it apart. The city's proximity to Tayrona National Park makes it the perfect base for exploring this ecological gem. Just a short drive away, Tayrona is a paradise of pristine beaches, dense jungles, and towering mountains that seem to rise directly from the sea. The park is home to a dazzling array of flora and fauna, including howler monkeys, toucans, and even elusive jaguars. Its biodiversity is matched only by its cultural significance, as the land is sacred to the indigenous Kogi,

Arhuaco, and Wiwa peoples who consider the Sierra Nevada de Santa Marta to be the "Heart of the World."

Visiting Tayrona National Park is an adventure in itself, requiring a bit of planning and preparation. The park's most famous beaches, such as Cabo San Juan and La Piscina, are accessible by hiking trails that wind through lush forests and offer stunning views of the coastline. The trails range in difficulty, but the effort is well worth it; there is nothing quite like emerging from the jungle to find yourself on a secluded beach, the turquoise waters lapping gently at the shore. For those who prefer a more leisurely approach, horseback riding is another option, allowing visitors to take in the scenery at a relaxed pace.

Accommodations within the park range from rustic campsites to eco-friendly lodges, offering something for every type of traveler. Spending a night in Tayrona is an unforgettable experience, as the lack of artificial light reveals a night sky filled with stars, and the sound of the waves provides a soothing soundtrack to your stay. The park's remote beauty and tranquility make it a place where time seems to stand still, allowing visitors to reconnect with nature and themselves.

Beyond Tayrona, the Sierra Nevada de Santa Marta offers even more opportunities for exploration. This mountain range, the highest coastal range in the world, is a UNESCO Biosphere Reserve and one of Colombia's most important ecological and cultural regions. The Lost City, or Ciudad Perdida, is perhaps its most famous attraction, an ancient archaeological site that predates Machu Picchu by several centuries. Reaching the Lost City requires a multi-day trek through challenging terrain, but the journey is as rewarding as the destination. Along the way, hikers encounter cascading waterfalls, indigenous villages, and breathtaking vistas that make the effort worthwhile.

Santa Marta itself offers plenty of opportunities to enjoy the Caribbean coastline without venturing too far afield. Rodadero Beach, located just a few kilometers from the city center, is a popular destination for both locals and tourists. Its golden sands and calm waters make it ideal for swimming, sunbathing, and water sports. For a quieter experience, Playa Blanca, accessible by boat, offers a more secluded setting with crystal-clear waters perfect for snorkeling. The nearby Taganga village, once a quiet fishing community, has become a hub for backpackers and scuba diving enthusiasts. Its laid-back atmosphere and stunning sunsets make it a favorite spot for those seeking a more bohemian vibe.

The culinary scene in Santa Marta reflects the region's coastal identity, with an emphasis on fresh seafood and tropical flavors. Dishes like ceviche, grilled fish, and coconut rice are staples, often accompanied by a refreshing limonada de coco, a local drink made from lime and coconut milk. Street food is also a highlight, with vendors offering treats like arepas, empanadas, and patacones. A visit to the Mercado Público provides a glimpse into the daily life of Santa Marta's residents, as well as an opportunity to sample the freshest produce and seafood the region has to offer.

The people of Santa Marta, known as samarios, are as warm and welcoming as the city's tropical climate. Their pride in their city and its natural surroundings is evident in every interaction, whether they are sharing stories about Tayrona or recommending their favorite local dishes. This sense of connection and community adds a personal dimension to any visit, making Santa Marta more than just a destination—it becomes an experience of hospitality and human connection.

Santa Marta's charm lies in its ability to offer something for everyone. History enthusiasts will find plenty to explore in its colonial landmarks and museums, while nature lovers will be captivated by the beauty of Tayrona and the Sierra Nevada. Those seeking relaxation can unwind on its beaches, while adventurers can challenge themselves with treks and dives. It is a city that invites you to slow down, to savor its flavors, its sights, and its stories, and to immerse yourself in the rhythm of the Caribbean.

What sets Santa Marta apart is its seamless blend of history and nature, its ability to connect the past with the present, and its role as a gateway to some of Colombia's most iconic landscapes. Whether you come for the beaches, the mountains, or the history, Santa Marta will leave an indelible mark on your heart. It is a city that invites you to explore, to discover, and to experience the very essence of Colombia's Caribbean coast.

## Bucaramanga: The City of Parks and Adventure

Bucaramanga, nestled in the northeastern Andean region of Colombia, is a city that often flies under the radar of international travelers, yet it holds treasures that easily rival its more famous counterparts. Known as the "City of Parks" for its abundance of green spaces, Bucaramanga is a harmonious blend of urban modernity and natural beauty. Its location, surrounded by lush mountains and deep canyons, makes it not only a serene city but also a hub for adventure tourism. With its mild climate, welcoming locals, and diverse offerings, Bucaramanga provides an experience that is both relaxing and exhilarating, a destination where nature and city life coexist seamlessly.

The parks of Bucaramanga are not merely decorative—they are living, breathing spaces where the city's rhythm unfolds. Parque García Rovira, situated in the heart of the city, is steeped in history and serves as a social hub for residents. Here, you'll find vendors selling snacks like obleas (thin wafers filled with caramel) and families enjoying the shade of ancient trees. Nearby, the imposing Cathedral of the Holy Family stands as a testament to Bucaramanga's colonial heritage, its neoclassical façade contrasting with the park's organic tranquility. It's a place where the past and present meet, where the city's pulse can be felt in every corner.

Another gem among Bucaramanga's many parks is Parque del Agua, an innovative space that combines recreation with environmental education. The park features a series of water-themed installations, including fountains, pools, and even a small stream that runs through its grounds. Designed to promote ecological awareness, it offers visitors the chance to learn about sustainable water use while enjoying its playful and serene atmosphere. Families flock here on weekends, drawn by the park's interactive exhibits and its peaceful ambiance, a reminder of Bucaramanga's commitment to preserving its natural surroundings.

For those seeking an elevated view of the city, Parque San Pío offers a quieter retreat, with its iconic statue by Colombian artist Fernando Botero providing a touch of artistic flair. The park's open spaces and well-maintained paths make it a favorite spot for joggers, dog walkers, and those simply looking to unwind. Each park in Bucaramanga offers something unique, collectively shaping the city into a green haven that invites both relaxation and reflection.

Beyond its parks, Bucaramanga is a gateway to some of Colombia's most stunning natural landscapes, making it a paradise for adventurers. Just an hour's drive from the city lies Chicamocha Canyon, a breathtaking natural wonder that stretches across the Santander region. This vast canyon, carved by the Chicamocha River over millennia, offers views that are nothing short of awe-inspiring. The Chicamocha National Park (Parque Nacional del Chicamocha), perched on the edge of the canyon, is a must-visit for those who crave both adventure and panoramic vistas. The park features a cable car that glides over the canyon, providing a bird's-eye view of its dramatic terrain, a sight that leaves most visitors speechless.

For thrill-seekers, Chicamocha offers activities that range from paragliding to zip-lining, providing an adrenaline rush against the backdrop of the canyon's rugged beauty. Paragliding in particular has become a signature experience in the region, drawing enthusiasts from around the world. Taking off from the canyon's edge, participants soar over its depths, the wind carrying them across a landscape that seems almost otherworldly. The sensation of flying over one of Colombia's most iconic landmarks is nothing short of exhilarating, a memory that lingers long after the flight is over.

Closer to Bucaramanga, the small town of Mesa de Los Santos offers another slice of adventure. Known for its coffee plantations and scenic hiking trails, it's a destination that combines outdoor activities with cultural immersion. Visitors can tour coffee farms, learning about the cultivation process while sampling some of the finest brews in the region. The trails around Mesa de Los Santos lead to viewpoints that overlook the canyon, each turn revealing a new perspective on the landscape. It's a place where time seems to slow down, where the simplicity of rural life offers a welcome contrast to the city's urban energy.

Bucaramanga's connection to adventure is not limited to its natural surroundings; the city itself is home to activities that cater to adrenaline junkies and casual explorers alike. The Ruitoque plateau, located just outside the city, has become a hotspot for extreme sports. Paragliding is particularly popular here, with expert instructors offering tandem flights that provide a unique perspective on Bucaramanga and its surroundings. The plateau's gentle winds and open spaces make it an ideal location for beginners, while the sweeping views of the city and the Andean foothills add an extra layer of magic to the experience.

For those who prefer their adventures on solid ground, the El Santísimo Ecopark offers a blend of outdoor exploration and cultural enrichment. The park's centerpiece is a towering statue of Christ, which can be reached via a cable car that offers stunning views of the surrounding landscape. Once at the top, visitors can enjoy walking trails, gardens, and an observation deck that provides a panoramic view of Bucaramanga and the Chicamocha Canyon in the distance. The park is a testament to the region's ability to combine natural beauty with thoughtful development, creating spaces that inspire both awe and reverence.

Bucaramanga's culinary scene is another facet of its charm, offering flavors that reflect the region's agricultural abundance and cultural heritage. The Santander region is known for unique dishes such as cabro (roasted goat) and pepitoria, a flavorful rice dish made with goat meat and offal. Street food is also a highlight, with options like empanadas santandereanas, filled with meat and potatoes, and hormigas culonas, or big-bottomed ants, a local delicacy that dates back to indigenous traditions. For a truly immersive experience, a visit to one of Bucaramanga's traditional markets, such as the Plaza de Mercado San Francisco, provides a chance to sample these dishes while mingling with locals.

The people of Bucaramanga, often called bumangueses, are known for their warmth and pride in their city. Their hospitality is evident in every interaction, whether it's a shopkeeper sharing recommendations or a guide explaining the history of the region. This sense of community is part of what makes Bucaramanga such a welcoming destination, a place where visitors quickly feel at home. The city's emphasis on quality of life, from its well-maintained parks to its thriving cultural scene, reflects the values of its residents, who take pride in preserving the beauty and vibrancy of their home.

What makes Bucaramanga truly special is its ability to offer something for everyone. Whether you're an outdoor enthusiast looking to explore the Chicamocha Canyon, a history buff drawn to its colonial heritage, or simply someone seeking a tranquil escape in one of its many parks, the city delivers an experience that is both enriching and unforgettable. Its blend of urban sophistication and natural splendor creates a destination that feels both dynamic and serene, a place where every visitor can find their own rhythm.

Bucaramanga is more than just a city; it's a gateway to adventure, a haven of green spaces, and a reflection of Colombia's rich diversity. Its parks and landscapes invite you to slow down and breathe, while its adventurous spirit challenges you to step out of your comfort zone. It's a city that surprises and delights at every turn, leaving a lasting impression on all who visit. For those seeking a destination that combines natural beauty, cultural depth, and a touch of excitement, Bucaramanga is a place that promises to deliver on every front.

# Popayán: Colombia's White City of Colonial Elegance

Popayán, often referred to as Colombia's White City, is a treasure trove of colonial elegance, history, and cultural depth. Nestled in the southwestern region of the country, this city has long been regarded as one of Colombia's most beautiful and culturally significant destinations. Its gleaming whitewashed facades, an enduring symbol of its colonial past, line the streets of its historic center, creating an atmosphere of timeless beauty and refinement. Beyond its striking architecture, Popayán is a city steeped in tradition, known for its deep religious roots, revered Semana Santa (Holy Week) celebrations, and a culinary heritage that has earned it recognition as a UNESCO City of Gastronomy. Exploring Popayán is like stepping into a living museum, where every plaza, church, and cobbled street tells a story of faith, resilience, and artistic expression.

The heart of Popayán lies in its historic center, a meticulously preserved district that reflects the city's colonial origins. Founded in 1537 by Spanish conquistador Sebastián de Belalcázar, Popayán quickly became a key political and economic hub during the colonial era. Its strategic location on the route between Cartagena and Quito made it a vital link in the Spanish Empire's trade network. The wealth generated during this period is evident in the city's grand churches, stately mansions, and ornate public buildings, all of which were constructed with a level of craftsmanship that continues to inspire admiration. Walking through the historic center, it's impossible not to be struck by the dazzling uniformity of its whitewashed walls, a tradition that dates back centuries and gives the city its nickname.

Among the architectural jewels of Popayán is the Iglesia de San Francisco, a stunning example of Baroque design. This church, completed in the 18th century, is one of the largest and most important religious structures in the city. Its intricately carved stone façade and soaring interior are a testament to the skill of the artisans who built it. Nearby, the

Capilla de Belén offers a more intimate experience, perched atop a hill that provides sweeping views of the city and its surroundings. This small chapel, with its simple yet elegant design, is a favorite spot for both locals and visitors seeking a moment of reflection.

The Catedral Basílica Nuestra Señora de la Asunción, located on the city's main square, Plaza de Caldas, is another iconic landmark. This neoclassical cathedral, rebuilt after a devastating earthquake in 1983, stands as a symbol of Popayán's resilience and faith. The plaza itself is a lively gathering place, surrounded by historic buildings such as the Torre del Reloj, or Clock Tower, which has stood as a sentinel over the city since the 17th century. The blend of historical grandeur and everyday activity makes Plaza de Caldas a microcosm of Popayán's enduring charm.

Popayán's religious heritage is perhaps most vividly expressed during Semana Santa, a tradition that has earned the city international recognition. The Holy Week processions, which date back to the 16th century, are among the oldest and most elaborate in Latin America. These processions, declared a UNESCO Intangible Cultural Heritage of Humanity, feature intricately crafted floats adorned with religious icons, flowers, and candles. Carried through the streets by devoted participants, these floats are accompanied by solemn music and prayers, creating a deeply moving spectacle that attracts pilgrims and tourists from around the world. The processions are a reflection of Popayán's spiritual identity, a city where faith and tradition are woven into the fabric of daily life.

The Semana Santa Museum, located in the historic center, provides an opportunity to delve deeper into the history and significance of these processions. The museum houses an impressive collection of religious artifacts, including the painstakingly preserved figures and ornaments used in the processions. Visitors can learn about the craftsmanship behind the floats, the symbolism of the rituals, and the efforts to preserve this centuries-old tradition. For those unable to experience Semana Santa firsthand, the museum offers a glimpse into the spiritual and cultural heart of Popayán.

Popayán's contributions to Colombian culture extend beyond religion and architecture; it is also a city of intellectual and artistic achievement. The city has produced numerous notable figures, including poets, writers, and politicians who have shaped the nation's history. The University of Cauca, one of Colombia's oldest and most prestigious institutions, has been a center of learning and innovation since its founding in 1827. Its campus, located in the historic center, is a hub of academic and cultural activity, hosting events, lectures, and exhibitions that reflect the city's vibrant intellectual life.

No visit to Popayán would be complete without exploring its culinary heritage, which has earned it the title of UNESCO City of Gastronomy. The city's cuisine is a reflection of its diverse cultural influences, blending indigenous, Spanish, and African traditions into a unique culinary identity. Traditional dishes such as empanadas de pipián, filled with a savory mixture of potatoes and peanuts, and tamales de pipián, wrapped in banana leaves, are staples of Popayán's food culture. Another must-try is the sopa de carantanta, a hearty soup made with dried corn husks, which showcases the resourcefulness and creativity of the region's cooks.

Popayán is also known for its desserts, which are often rooted in colonial-era recipes. Manjar blanco, a sweet, creamy delicacy similar to dulce de leche, is a local favorite, often enjoyed with wafers or as a filling for pastries. The city's markets, such as Mercado Bolívar, are treasure troves of these culinary delights, offering visitors the chance to sample traditional flavors while interacting with local vendors. Dining in Popayán is not just about satisfying hunger; it's an opportunity to connect with the city's history and traditions through its food.

The natural beauty surrounding Popayán adds another dimension to its appeal. The nearby Puracé National Park, located just a short drive from the city, is a haven for nature lovers and adventure seekers. This park, named after the active Puracé Volcano, is part of the Andean mountain range and features diverse ecosystems ranging from cloud forests to high-altitude páramos. Hiking trails lead visitors through breathtaking landscapes, where they can encounter waterfalls, thermal springs, and unique wildlife such as the Andean condor. The park's proximity to Popayán makes it an ideal destination for a day trip, offering a stark contrast to the urban elegance of the White City.

Popayán's charm lies in its ability to balance its rich cultural heritage with a sense of modernity and accessibility. Despite its historical significance, the city feels alive and dynamic, a place where traditions are not just preserved but actively celebrated. Its residents, known as payaneses, are proud of their city and eager to share its stories, whether through guided tours, cultural events, or simple conversations over a cup of tinto, Colombia's ubiquitous black coffee.

What sets Popayán apart is its ability to transport visitors to a different time while remaining firmly rooted in the present. Its whitewashed walls, grand churches, and cobblestone streets evoke the colonial era, yet its vibrant cultural scene and culinary innovations remind us that it is a city that continues to evolve. Whether you're drawn to its architectural beauty, its religious traditions, or its culinary delights, Popayán offers an experience that is as enriching as it is unforgettable. It is a city that invites exploration, reflection, and a deeper appreciation of Colombia's diverse cultural landscape.

## Pereira and Manizales: Discovering the Coffee Triangle's Urban Gems

Pereira and Manizales, two of the most prominent cities in Colombia's Coffee Triangle, offer a fascinating blend of urban energy, cultural richness, and the serene beauty of their surrounding landscapes. Nestled among the verdant coffee plantations that give the region its name, these cities serve as gateways to one of the most celebrated coffee-growing regions in the world. While the Coffee Triangle—or Eje Cafetero—is often associated with its lush fincas and rural charm, Pereira and Manizales add a distinctly urban dimension to the experience. These cities are not merely stopping points; they are thriving hubs of culture, history, and innovation, deeply intertwined with the coffee culture that defines the region.

Pereira, the largest city in the Coffee Triangle, is a dynamic urban center that balances its rapid growth with a strong connection to its agricultural roots. Founded in 1863, Pereira has long been a commercial and transportation hub, strategically located at the crossroads of Colombia's central Andes. Its location has made it a melting pot of cultures and ideas, fostering a spirit of entrepreneurship and creativity that permeates the city today. Walking through Pereira, you'll notice a juxtaposition of modernity and tradition: sleek office buildings and shopping malls stand alongside bustling mercados and coffee shops where locals gather for lively conversations over a perfectly brewed tinto.

At the heart of Pereira is Plaza de Bolívar, a lively square dominated by the iconic Bolívar Desnudo statue. This striking bronze sculpture, depicting Simón Bolívar in an unconventional pose, is both a symbol of the city's progressive spirit and a point of pride for its residents. Surrounding the plaza are historic buildings and shaded walkways, making it a popular meeting place for locals and tourists alike. From here, you can explore the city's vibrant streets, which are lined with boutiques, cafes, and restaurants offering both traditional and contemporary cuisine. Pereira's culinary scene is deeply influenced by its coffee culture, with many establishments showcasing innovative uses of coffee in both food and beverages.

One of Pereira's most cherished landmarks is the Viaducto César Gaviria Trujillo, a stunning cable-stayed bridge that connects the city to neighboring Dosquebradas. Named after a former Colombian president, the bridge is not only an engineering marvel but also a symbol of the city's growth and connectivity. Walking or driving across the viaduct offers sweeping views of the surrounding mountains and valleys, a reminder of the natural beauty that envelops the city. Pereira's commitment to infrastructure and development is evident in projects like this, which have helped transform it into a modern, accessible city while maintaining its connection to the Coffee Triangle's rural charm.

For those seeking a deeper connection to Pereira's coffee heritage, a visit to one of the nearby coffee farms is a must. Just a short drive from the city, you'll find fincas that offer guided tours, allowing visitors to learn about the coffee production process from bean to cup. These tours often include hands-on activities, such as picking coffee cherries or roasting beans, as well as opportunities to sample freshly brewed coffee in idyllic settings. The experience provides a tangible link to the region's agricultural traditions and highlights the care and craftsmanship that go into producing some of the world's finest coffee.

Manizales, located to the north of Pereira, offers a different yet equally captivating perspective on life in the Coffee Triangle. Perched on a ridge at an elevation of over 2,000 meters (6,562 feet), Manizales is often referred to as the "City of Open Doors" for its reputation as one of the friendliest cities in Colombia. Its high altitude provides cooler temperatures and stunning views of the surrounding mountains, including the snow-capped peaks of the Nevado del Ruiz volcano. This striking backdrop lends Manizales a sense of grandeur and tranquility that is hard to match.

The city's historic center, with its narrow streets and colonial architecture, exudes a timeless charm. One of its most iconic landmarks is the Manizales Cathedral, or Catedral Basílica Nuestra Señora del Rosario, a towering neo-Gothic structure that dominates the skyline. The cathedral's interior is as impressive as its exterior, with intricate stained-glass windows and soaring arches that inspire awe. For the adventurous, the cathedral offers a guided tour of its rooftop, where you can enjoy panoramic views of the city and its surroundings. The experience is both thrilling and humbling, a reminder of Manizales' unique position between the heavens and the earth.

Manizales is also known for its vibrant cultural scene, which is deeply influenced by the city's academic heritage. Home to several universities, including the prestigious Universidad de Caldas, Manizales has a youthful energy that fuels its festivals, arts, and nightlife. The annual Manizales Fair, held every January, is one of the city's most anticipated events, featuring parades, concerts, bullfights, and cultural exhibitions that celebrate the region's traditions. The fair attracts visitors from across Colombia and beyond, transforming the city into a kaleidoscope of color, music, and excitement.

One of the unique aspects of Manizales is its proximity to the Nevados National Park, a natural wonderland that offers endless opportunities for exploration and adventure. The park is home to a range of ecosystems, from cloud forests to high-altitude páramos, as well as the majestic Nevado del Ruiz volcano. Guided tours of the park allow visitors to hike its trails, observe its diverse flora and fauna, and even experience thermal hot springs fed by volcanic activity. The park's otherworldly landscapes are a stark contrast to the urban charm of Manizales, offering a chance to reconnect with nature in one of Colombia's most spectacular settings.

Manizales' connection to the coffee culture of the region is as strong as Pereira's, with numerous fincas located just outside the city. These farms not only produce high-quality coffee but also serve as centers of innovation and sustainability, experimenting with new cultivation methods and eco-friendly practices. Many of these fincas welcome visitors, offering tours that delve into the science and art of coffee production. Whether you're a casual coffee drinker or a connoisseur, spending time at a finca is an enriching experience that deepens your appreciation for the work that goes into every cup.

Both Pereira and Manizales are cities that embody the spirit of the Coffee Triangle in their own unique ways. Pereira, with its modern infrastructure and entrepreneurial energy, represents the dynamic future of the region, while Manizales, with its historic charm and cultural vibrancy, offers a glimpse into its storied past. Together, they provide a comprehensive picture of life in the Coffee Triangle, where urban sophistication and rural traditions coexist in harmony.

The people of these cities, known for their warmth and hospitality, are an integral part of what makes them so special. Whether you're sharing a cup of coffee with a local farmer, exploring the bustling streets of Pereira, or marveling at the views from Manizales, you'll encounter a sense of pride and community that is deeply rooted in the region's identity. This connection to the land, the culture, and each other is what sets the Coffee Triangle apart, making it a destination that stays with you long after you leave.

Pereira and Manizales are more than just urban centers; they are living reflections of the Coffee Triangle's rich heritage and promising future. Their landscapes, traditions, and people come together to create an experience that is as complex and rewarding as the coffee they produce. Whether you're drawn to the energy of Pereira, the charm of Manizales, or the natural beauty that surrounds them, these cities offer an unforgettable journey into the heart of Colombia's coffee culture.

# CHAPTER 2: EXPLORING COLOMBIA'S NATURAL WONDERS

## Tayrona National Park: Beaches, Jungle, and Adventure

Tayrona National Park, located on Colombia's northern Caribbean coast, is a natural sanctuary where the raw beauty of beaches, jungle, and mountains collide to create an extraordinary landscape. Spanning 150 square kilometers of protected land, the park is a haven of biodiversity and cultural significance, offering some of the most breathtaking scenery in the country. It is a place where turquoise waters lap against golden sands, dense forests hum with the sounds of wildlife, and ancient indigenous traditions remain deeply rooted in the land. Tayrona is not just a destination—it is an immersive experience that invites visitors to reconnect with nature and explore a world that feels untouched by time.

The first thing that strikes you upon entering Tayrona National Park is the sheer diversity of its ecosystems. The park's geography is shaped by its proximity to the towering Sierra Nevada de Santa Marta, the world's highest coastal mountain range. This unique setting creates a dramatic contrast between the lush greenery of the jungle and the sparkling expanse of the Caribbean Sea. Within Tayrona's boundaries, you'll find everything from tropical rainforests and mangroves to coral reefs and arid scrublands. Each ecosystem supports a wide array of flora and fauna, making the park a paradise for nature enthusiasts. Over 300 species of birds call Tayrona home, along with monkeys, iguanas, and even jaguars, though the latter are elusive and rarely seen.

The park's beaches are undoubtedly its most famous feature, drawing visitors from around the world with their postcard-perfect beauty. Cabo San Juan, perhaps the most iconic of these beaches, is a crescent-shaped stretch of sand framed by giant boulders and swaying palm trees. Its calm, clear waters make it an ideal spot for swimming and snorkeling, while the surrounding jungle adds an air of seclusion and tranquility. Reaching Cabo San Juan requires a hike through the park's dense forest, which only heightens the sense of discovery as you emerge onto the beach. Along the way, the trail offers glimpses of other pristine beaches, such as Arrecifes and La Piscina, each with its own unique charm.

Despite their beauty, some of Tayrona's beaches carry an element of danger, with strong currents and riptides that make them unsuitable for swimming. Signs posted along the trails clearly indicate which areas are safe, and it's crucial to heed these warnings. For those who prefer to stay on land, the beaches offer plenty of opportunities for relaxation, whether it's sunbathing on the warm sand, exploring tide pools teeming with marine life, or simply soaking in the views of the endless horizon. The sound of the waves, the rustle of the palms, and the calls of distant birds combine to create an ambiance of pure serenity.

Venturing beyond the beaches, Tayrona's jungle trails offer a completely different kind of adventure. The park's network of hiking paths winds through dense forests, where sunlight filters through the canopy in dappled patterns and the air is thick with the scent of earth and vegetation. These trails vary in difficulty, ranging from easy walks suitable for families to more challenging treks that require stamina and proper footwear. Along the way, hikers encounter hidden waterfalls, ancient trees with sprawling roots, and occasional wildlife sightings. The jungle feels alive, its sounds and movements creating a symphony that accompanies you on your journey.

One of the most intriguing aspects of Tayrona is its cultural heritage, which is closely tied to the indigenous communities that have lived in the region for centuries. The park is considered sacred by the Kogi, Arhuaco, Wiwa, and Kankuamo peoples, who see the Sierra Nevada de Santa Marta as the "Heart of the World." These communities maintain a spiritual connection to the land, viewing it as a living entity that must be protected and respected. Visitors may encounter indigenous people dressed in traditional white clothing, often on their way to or from ceremonial sites. While their presence adds a sense of reverence to the park, it's important to approach them with respect and avoid intruding on their privacy.

One of the most significant cultural sites within Tayrona is Pueblito, an ancient archaeological site that offers a glimpse into the lives of the indigenous Tayrona civilization that once thrived here. Pueblito, also known as Chairama, is thought to have been a major settlement, and its stone terraces, pathways, and ceremonial structures hint at the complexity of its society. Reaching Pueblito requires a strenuous hike, but the journey is as rewarding as the destination. The trail passes through rugged terrain, offering stunning views of the surrounding mountains and coastline. Standing among the ruins, you can't help but feel a sense of awe at the ingenuity of the Tayrona people, who built this settlement in harmony with the natural landscape.

Accommodations within Tayrona National Park range from rustic campsites to eco-friendly lodges, allowing visitors to choose how deeply they wish to immerse themselves in the natural environment. Camping is a popular option, particularly at Cabo San Juan, where tents can be rented, and hammocks are available for those who prefer to sleep under the stars. The experience of waking up to the sound of waves and the sight of the sun rising over the Caribbean is one that stays with you long after you leave. For those seeking more comfort, the park also offers lodges that blend sustainable design with modern amenities, providing a cozy retreat after a day of exploration.

The park's marine environment is just as captivating as its terrestrial landscapes, making it a haven for water-based activities. Snorkeling is a favorite pastime, particularly at La Piscina and Cabo San Juan, where the clear waters reveal vibrant coral reefs and schools of tropical fish. Scuba diving is another option, with dive operators offering excursions to sites just outside the park's boundaries. These underwater adventures provide a closer look at the rich marine biodiversity of the Caribbean, from colorful parrotfish and angelfish to elusive sea turtles.

Tayrona's appeal lies in its ability to offer something for everyone, whether you're seeking relaxation, adventure, or a deeper connection to nature and culture. Families can enjoy leisurely walks and safe swimming areas, while thrill-seekers can tackle challenging hikes or dive into the underwater world. The park's blend of natural beauty and cultural significance creates a sense of harmony that is both inspiring and humbling. It's a place where the modern world feels distant, where time slows down, and where every moment feels infused with the magic of the natural world.

To fully appreciate Tayrona, it's essential to approach it with a sense of responsibility and respect. The park's fragile ecosystems and cultural heritage depend on thoughtful stewardship, both by its caretakers and its visitors. Simple actions, such as staying on marked trails, avoiding littering, and respecting the privacy of indigenous communities, go a long way in preserving this remarkable place for future generations. Tayrona is not just a destination to be consumed; it's a living, breathing entity that deserves to be cherished and protected.

Leaving Tayrona is never easy. The memories of its golden beaches, emerald jungles, and tranquil sunsets linger long after you've returned to the hustle and bustle of daily life. It's a place that has a way of staying with you, reminding you of the beauty and interconnectedness of the natural world. For many, a visit to Tayrona is not just a vacation—it's a transformative experience, one that deepens your appreciation for the planet and your place within it.

# The Amazon Rainforest: A Journey into Biodiversity

The Amazon Rainforest, often referred to as the "lungs of the Earth," is a world of unparalleled biodiversity and breathtaking natural beauty. Spanning nine countries and covering approximately 5.5 million square kilometers, it is the largest rainforest on the planet. Colombia, home to a significant portion of the Amazon Basin, offers a gateway into this awe-inspiring ecosystem. Beyond its staggering size, the Amazon is a place of profound ecological importance, a sanctuary for countless species of plants and animals, and a vital resource for the health of our planet. In Colombia, the Amazon reveals itself in all its raw magnificence, inviting travelers to explore its dense canopies, winding rivers, and the vibrant cultures that have existed in harmony with the forest for centuries.

The journey into the Colombian Amazon often begins in Leticia, a remote town nestled along the banks of the Amazon River, where Colombia meets Brazil and Peru. Leticia serves as the main entry point to the rainforest, a small yet lively hub that hums with the rhythms of river life. Boats of every size line the docks, carrying goods, passengers, and supplies up and down the river. The air is thick with humidity and the scent of wet earth, mingled with the aroma of freshly cooked fish from open-air kitchens. At first glance, Leticia may seem like a bustling outpost, but it quickly becomes clear that it is much more than a gateway—it is a place where urban life and the wild Amazon coexist in delicate balance.

Leticia's Mercado Municipal is a kaleidoscope of sights, sounds, and smells, offering a glimpse into the daily lives of the region's inhabitants. Vendors hawk exotic fruits like camu camu and copoazú, their brightly colored skins a stark contrast against the earthy tones of the market stalls. Fresh fish from the river glisten on tables, while baskets of cassava and local spices emit a heady aroma. The market is also a cultural crossroads, where indigenous communities, river dwellers, and travelers converge. It is the perfect place to sample Amazonian flavors, from pirarucú, a massive freshwater fish, to juanes, rice and meat wrapped in banana leaves.

From Leticia, the Amazon River stretches out like a lifeline, its muddy waters winding through the dense greenery of the rainforest. The river is both a highway and a source of sustenance, supporting the communities that live along its banks. Traveling by boat is the primary way to navigate this vast and intricate world. Wooden canoes and motorized launches glide silently past the towering trees, their roots dipping into the water as if to drink from the river's flow. Along the way, you might spot pink river dolphins breaking the surface, their playful movements adding a touch of magic to the already surreal landscape. The river is alive, its currents carrying not just water, but stories, traditions, and the pulse of the Amazon.

One of the most striking aspects of the Amazon Rainforest is its staggering biodiversity. The sheer variety of life here is almost incomprehensible, with the region hosting over 400 billion individual trees, representing thousands of species. The rainforest is home to jaguars, sloths, howler monkeys, and an astonishing array of birds, including the vibrant macaws and toucans that flash through the canopy. The forest floor, often shrouded in shadows, teems with insects, amphibians, and smaller mammals, while the rivers and oxbow lakes harbor caimans, piranhas, and giant river otters. The Amazon is a living laboratory, its ecosystems so complex that scientists are still discovering new species with every expedition.

Exploring the rainforest itself is an experience that defies comparison. Guided treks take visitors deep into the heart of the jungle, where the sounds of civilization fade away, replaced by the symphony of the forest. Cicadas drone in the background, while the calls of birds echo through the trees. The air is heavy with moisture, and sunlight filters through the canopy in golden beams, illuminating the intricate patterns of leaves and vines. Walking through this dense greenery, you quickly realize that the Amazon is not just a collection of trees—it is an interconnected web of life, each organism playing a role in the delicate balance of the ecosystem.

Indigenous communities are an integral part of the Amazon's identity, their lives deeply intertwined with the rhythms of the forest. In Colombia, tribes such as the Ticuna, Huitoto, and Yagua have lived in harmony with the rainforest for generations, their knowledge of the land surpassing anything found in textbooks. Many communities welcome visitors, offering a chance to learn about their traditions, beliefs, and sustainable practices. These encounters are not only educational but also deeply humbling, as they reveal a way of life that prioritizes respect for nature and a sense of interconnectedness with the world.

A visit to a maloca, or traditional communal house, provides insight into the spiritual and social fabric of Amazonian culture. These large, thatched-roof structures serve as gathering places for ceremonies, storytelling, and decision-making. Inside, the air is thick with the scent of wood and earth, and the walls are adorned with symbols and carvings that represent the tribe's cosmology. Listening to an elder recount myths of creation or explain the significance of medicinal plants is a profound experience, one that bridges the gap between ancient wisdom and modern curiosity.

One of the most enchanting aspects of the Amazon is its night sky. Away from the light pollution of cities, the stars shine with a brilliance that is difficult to describe. As the forest settles into its nocturnal rhythms, the sounds of the night take over—frogs croak, crickets chirp, and the occasional rustle of leaves hints at unseen creatures moving through the undergrowth. Staring up at the vast expanse of the Milky Way, it's impossible not to feel a sense of wonder and connection to something greater.

For those seeking adventure, the Amazon offers countless opportunities to engage with its untamed beauty. Kayaking through flooded forests, known as várzeas, allows you to glide silently among submerged trees, their trunks rising like ghostly sentinels from the water. Fishing for piranhas is another thrilling activity, combining patience with a touch of daring. Canopy walks, where suspended bridges allow you to traverse the treetops, provide a bird's-eye view of the forest and its inhabitants. Each activity offers a different perspective on the Amazon, revealing its many layers and secrets.

The challenges facing the Amazon Rainforest cannot be ignored. Deforestation, illegal mining, and climate change pose significant threats to this vital ecosystem. However, efforts are underway to protect and preserve the region, from government initiatives to grassroots movements led by indigenous communities. Tourism, when approached responsibly, can play a role in these efforts by providing economic support to local communities and raising awareness about the importance of conservation. Visitors to the Amazon are not just passive observers—they become part of a larger story, one that emphasizes the need to protect this irreplaceable treasure.

Leaving the Amazon is a bittersweet experience. The memories of its vibrant colors, its intoxicating scents, and its symphony of sounds linger long after you've returned to the modern world. It is a place that defies expectations, challenging you to see the world through new eyes and to recognize the intricate connections that bind all living things. The Amazon is not just a destination—it is a reminder of the planet's resilience, its fragility, and its boundless capacity to inspire.

## The Cocora Valley: Home of the World's Tallest Palm Trees

The Cocora Valley, nestled in Colombia's Quindío department, is a place of surreal beauty, where towering wax palms—the tallest palm trees in the world—rise elegantly into the sky, their slender trunks piercing through the clouds. This enchanting valley is part of the larger Los Nevados National Natural Park, a sprawling protected area that showcases the diverse ecosystems of Colombia's Andean region. Walking through the Cocora Valley feels like stepping into a dreamscape, with its rolling green hills, mist-shrouded peaks, and the striking silhouettes of the wax palms creating an unforgettable visual tapestry. Beyond its natural allure, the valley is an ecological treasure, home to unique flora and fauna and a vital component of Colombia's cultural and environmental heritage.

The wax palm, or Ceroxylon quindiuense, is not only a striking feature of the landscape but also Colombia's national tree.

Growing to heights of up to 60 meters (almost 200 feet), these graceful giants have adapted to thrive in the high-altitude cloud forests of the Andes. Their smooth, wax-coated trunks are a pale gray, and their fronds form crowns that sway gently in the wind, creating a mesmerizing dance against the backdrop of the valley's emerald slopes. These trees were once harvested for their wax, which was used to make candles, but today they are a protected species, recognized for their ecological importance and their role as a symbol of Colombia's natural beauty.

The journey to the Cocora Valley often begins in the nearby town of Salento, a charming pueblo known for its brightly painted houses, artisan shops, and welcoming atmosphere. Salento serves as the perfect base for exploring the valley, with its cobblestone streets and bustling plaza offering a taste of traditional Colombian life. Jeeps, known locally as "Willys," line the square, ready to ferry visitors to the valley's entrance. These vintage vehicles, a relic of Colombia's agricultural past, are as much a part of the experience as the destination itself. The ride to the Cocora Valley is a thrilling adventure, with the jeep bouncing along winding mountain roads as the scenery becomes increasingly dramatic.

Arriving at the entrance to the valley, visitors are immediately greeted by a sense of tranquility and wonder. The air is cooler here, carrying the faint scent of damp earth and vegetation. Hiking trails fan out from the entrance, offering a range of options for exploring the landscape. The most popular route is a loop trail that takes hikers through the heart of the valley, offering a mix of open meadows, dense cloud forests, and panoramic viewpoints. The trail is well-marked but can be challenging in places, with steep inclines and muddy sections that require sturdy footwear and a bit of perseverance.

One of the highlights of the hike is the opportunity to see the wax palms up close. Standing beneath these towering trees, you can't help but feel a sense of awe at their scale and elegance. Their trunks seem to stretch endlessly upward, disappearing into the mist, while their fronds form delicate patterns against the sky. The interplay of light and shadow creates a constantly shifting canvas, with the trees casting long, dramatic silhouettes as the sun moves across the valley. This is a place where time seems to slow down, allowing you to fully immerse yourself in the beauty of the natural world.

As you ascend the trail, the landscape begins to change, transitioning from open pastures to dense cloud forest. The forest is alive with the sounds of birds, insects, and rustling leaves, creating a symphony that accompanies you on your journey. The air grows cooler and more humid, and the trail becomes narrower, winding its way through a tangle of ferns, moss-covered trees, and hanging vines. This section of the hike offers a glimpse into the valley's incredible biodiversity, with every step revealing new textures, colors, and shapes. It's a reminder of the intricate connections that sustain life in this fragile ecosystem.

The cloud forest is also home to a remarkable array of wildlife, much of which is endemic to the region. Birdwatchers, in particular, will find the Cocora Valley to be a paradise, with species such as the Andean condor, the yellow-eared parrot, and the multicolored tanager frequently spotted in the area. The yellow-eared parrot, once critically endangered due to habitat loss, has made a remarkable recovery thanks to conservation efforts in the Cocora Valley and surrounding areas. Seeing these vibrant birds perched among the wax palms is a powerful reminder of the importance of protecting these habitats for future generations.

One of the most rewarding stops along the trail is the Acaime Reserve, a small sanctuary that offers a chance to rest, refuel, and observe the valley's famous hummingbirds. These tiny, iridescent creatures flit from flower to flower, their wings beating so rapidly that they appear to hover in mid-air. The reserve provides feeders filled with sugar water, attracting a dazzling array of species that seem almost otherworldly in their beauty. Sitting on the reserve's wooden benches, sipping a hot cup of aguapanela (a traditional Colombian drink made from sugarcane), and watching the hummingbirds dart and dive is a moment of pure serenity.

The Cocora Valley is not only a haven for nature lovers but also a place of deep cultural significance. The indigenous Quimbaya people, who once inhabited this region, held the wax palm in high regard, considering it a sacred tree that connected the earth to the heavens. Today, the valley continues to hold spiritual meaning for many Colombians, serving as a symbol of the country's resilience and natural heritage. The wax palms, with their improbable height and enduring presence, are a testament to the strength and adaptability of life in the face of challenges.

For those who prefer a less strenuous experience, horseback riding is another popular way to explore the valley. Local guides offer tours that take visitors along the trails, providing insight into the region's history, ecology, and traditions. Riding through the valley on horseback allows you to cover more ground while enjoying the scenery at a leisurely pace. The rhythm of the horse's gait, combined with the sounds of the forest and the sight of the wax palms, creates a deeply immersive experience that feels almost timeless.

As the day draws to a close and the light begins to fade, the valley takes on a different character. The golden hues of sunset bathe the landscape in warmth, casting long shadows that stretch across the hills. The wax palms, silhouetted against the vibrant colors of the sky, seem to stand even taller, their forms etched into the memory like a living work of art. It's a moment that captures the essence of the Cocora Valley—a place where nature's beauty and grandeur are on full display, leaving an indelible impression on all who visit.

The Cocora Valley is more than just a destination; it is a sanctuary for the soul, a place where the wonders of the natural world inspire both awe and reflection. Its landscapes are a reminder of the importance of preserving the delicate balance of our planet's ecosystems, while its cultural and historical significance adds depth to its allure. Whether you're hiking through the cloud forest, marveling at the wax palms, or simply sitting in quiet contemplation, the Cocora Valley offers an experience that is as enriching as it is unforgettable.

It is a place that stays with you long after you've left, its beauty and spirit lingering in your heart and mind.

## The Guajira Peninsula: Desert Landscapes and Indigenous Culture

The Guajira Peninsula, located at the northernmost tip of South America, is a land of contrasts, where harsh desert landscapes meet the azure waters of the Caribbean Sea. This remote and rugged region is unlike any other in Colombia, offering a stark beauty that captivates the soul and a deep cultural richness rooted in the traditions of the Wayuu people, the peninsula's indigenous inhabitants. The Guajira Peninsula is a place where the wind carries the whispers of ancient stories, where sand dunes stretch endlessly toward the horizon, and where life thrives against all odds in one of the most arid environments in the country. It is a destination that challenges, inspires, and leaves an indelible mark on those who journey there.

The journey to the Guajira Peninsula begins in Riohacha, the region's capital and main gateway. This coastal town, with its palm-lined beaches and bustling boardwalk, serves as the starting point for most expeditions into the peninsula's heart. Vendors line the Malecón, offering handmade Wayuu crafts, from intricately woven mochilas (bags) to hammocks in vibrant colors and patterns that reflect the cultural heritage of the region. Riohacha is a town that moves to its own rhythm, with the sound of waves mingling with the chatter of locals and the hum of motorcycles, the primary mode of transport here. It's a place where tradition and modernity coexist, offering a glimpse into the character of the Guajira region.

As you venture deeper into the peninsula, the landscape begins to transform. The lush greenery of the coast gives way to a stark and stunning desert, where towering cacti stand like sentinels and the earth shifts to shades of ochre, gold, and rust. The sun blazes overhead, and the wind carries fine grains of sand that shimmer in the light. The road, often unpaved and rugged, winds through this unforgiving terrain, dotted with small Wayuu settlements where life continues much as it has for centuries. These villages, with their simple thatched-roof huts known as rancherías, are a testament to the resilience and resourcefulness of the Wayuu people, who have adapted to this harsh environment through generations of ingenuity.

One of the most iconic destinations in the Guajira Peninsula is Cabo de la Vela, a remote fishing village that has become a symbol of the region's beauty and cultural significance. Cabo de la Vela's charm lies in its simplicity: a few humble lodgings, small family-run restaurants, and endless views of the Caribbean Sea meeting the desert sands. The village is a place to disconnect from the modern world and reconnect with nature, where the pace of life slows to the rhythm of the tides. Visitors often stay in traditional chinchorros, large hammocks strung up in open-air shelters that allow the sea breeze to lull them to sleep under a canopy of stars.

The beaches of Cabo de la Vela are unlike any others in Colombia. Playa Ojo de Agua, with its gentle waves and golden sands, is perfect for swimming and relaxing, while Playa del Pilón de Azúcar, named for the nearby sugarloaf-shaped hill, offers a more dramatic setting. The climb to the top of Pilón de Azúcar rewards visitors with panoramic views of the surrounding desert and sea, a breathtaking sight that captures the essence of the Guajira Peninsula. The contrast between the turquoise waters and the arid landscape creates a sense of otherworldly beauty, a reminder of the power and resilience of nature.

The Wayuu people, the largest indigenous group in Colombia, are the heart and soul of the Guajira Peninsula. Their culture, steeped in oral traditions, mythology, and a deep connection to the land, is an integral part of the region's identity. The Wayuu are a matrilineal society, with women playing key roles in both family and community life. Their art, particularly their weaving, is a form of storytelling, with each mochila bag, hammock, or piece of clothing bearing patterns that represent the natural world, dreams, and ancestral knowledge. Purchasing a Wayuu-made item is not just acquiring a souvenir; it is supporting a tradition that has been passed down through generations and preserving a piece of living history.

Visiting a Wayuu ranchería is an opportunity to learn more about their way of life. Many communities welcome visitors and offer cultural experiences that include traditional music, dance, and food. The Wayuu cuisine, shaped by the arid environment, is simple yet flavorful. Goat, or chivo, is a staple of their diet, often cooked in a hearty stew or roasted over an open flame. Friche, a dish made from goat meat seasoned with local spices, is a must-try for anyone exploring the region. Meals are often accompanied by yuca or plantains, staples that reflect the resourcefulness of the Wayuu people in cultivating food in such challenging conditions.

Further into the Guajira Peninsula lies Punta Gallinas, the northernmost point of South America and a place of almost mythical allure. Reaching Punta Gallinas is an adventure in itself, requiring a journey by 4x4 vehicle across vast stretches of desert and through salt flats that shimmer under the sun. The reward for this effort is a landscape of unparalleled beauty, where golden sand dunes spill into the emerald waters of the Caribbean. This remote and windswept corner of the peninsula is a place of solitude and reflection, where the only sounds are the whisper of the wind and the gentle lapping of waves.

The Taroa Dunes, located near Punta Gallinas, are among the most striking features of the Guajira Peninsula. These massive sand dunes rise dramatically from the sea, creating a surreal landscape that feels like something out of a dream. Climbing to the top of a dune and watching the sun set over the Caribbean is a moment of pure magic, a reminder of the vastness and beauty of the natural world. The dunes are constantly shifting, shaped by the wind and tides, a testament to the ever-changing nature of the Guajira region.

The Guajira Peninsula is also home to unique ecological features, including salt flats, mangroves, and lagoons that support a surprising diversity of wildlife. Flamingos, with their vibrant pink feathers, can often be seen wading in the shallow waters of the Los Flamencos Sanctuary, a protected area near the town of Camarones. This sanctuary is a haven for birdwatchers, with dozens of species making their home in the area's wetlands. The sight of flamingos silhouetted against the golden light of sunrise is one of the many unforgettable images the Guajira Peninsula offers.

Despite its beauty and cultural richness, the Guajira Peninsula faces significant challenges. Climate change, overexploitation of natural resources, and social inequalities have placed pressure on the region and its people. The Wayuu, in particular, have struggled with issues such as water scarcity and access to basic services. Tourism, when approached responsibly, can play a role in supporting the region by providing income for local communities and raising awareness about the importance of preserving this unique corner of the world. Travelers to the Guajira Peninsula have a responsibility to respect the land, its people, and their traditions, ensuring that their visit leaves a positive impact.

The Guajira Peninsula is a place that defies expectations and leaves a lasting impression. Its rugged landscapes, vibrant culture, and the resilience of its people create a destination that is as inspiring as it is humbling. Whether you're watching the sunrise over the Taroa Dunes, sharing a meal with a Wayuu family, or simply standing in awe of the desert meeting the sea, the Guajira Peninsula offers moments of profound connection to both nature and humanity. It is a journey into the heart of a land that is as unforgiving as it is beautiful, a place where the spirit of the desert and the soul of its people shine brightly.

# Caño Cristales: The River of Five Colors

Caño Cristales, often referred to as the "River of Five Colors" or the "Liquid Rainbow," is a natural phenomenon so vivid and otherworldly that it almost defies belief. Tucked away in the Serranía de la Macarena National Natural Park in central Colombia, this extraordinary river is celebrated for its dazzling display of colors that transform its waters into a living painting. Shades of red, yellow, green, blue, and black ripple across its surface, creating a spectacle that has earned it a place among the most beautiful rivers in the world. But Caño Cristales is much more than its kaleidoscopic appearance; it is a delicate ecosystem, a symbol of Colombia's environmental wealth, and an unforgettable destination for those fortunate enough to visit.

The river owes its stunning colors to an aquatic plant known as *Macarenia clavigera*, a species of algae that thrives in the unique conditions of the riverbed. During the wet and dry seasons, this plant undergoes a transformation, producing brilliant hues that range from deep crimson to bright pink. The phenomenon occurs between June and November, when the water levels are just right—not too high to obscure the plants, and not too low to dry them out. During this time, sunlight penetrates the crystal-clear water, illuminating the plants and creating the vibrant display that has captivated visitors and scientists alike. The interplay of sunlight, water, and the *Macarenia clavigera* is a delicate balance, one that underscores the fragility of this natural wonder.

Exploring the region begins in the small town of La Macarena, the main gateway to Caño Cristales. This quiet, unassuming town is surrounded by lush greenery and serves as the base for most visitors' excursions into the national park. La Macarena exudes a sense of warmth and hospitality, with its friendly residents eager to share the beauty of their homeland. Here, local guides, many of whom are deeply familiar with the area's ecology and history, play an essential role in ensuring that visitors experience the river responsibly. The town itself is a testament to the resilience of the region, which has emerged from decades of conflict to become a beacon of sustainable tourism and conservation.

Reaching Caño Cristales is an adventure in itself. From La Macarena, visitors typically travel by boat along the Guayabero River, a journey that offers its own quiet charms. The riverbanks are alive with activity, from the calls of tropical birds to the occasional sighting of monkeys swinging through the trees. The journey continues on foot or by horseback, as motorized vehicles are prohibited within the park to minimize environmental impact. As you approach the river, the anticipation builds, and the first glimpse of its vibrant colors is nothing short of breathtaking. The vivid hues seem almost unreal, a natural masterpiece unfolding before your eyes.

The river is not a single, continuous stretch of color but a series of pools, waterfalls, and rapids, each with its own unique character. Los Ochos, a set of circular rock formations, is one of the most photographed spots along the river, its natural pools glowing with a deep red hue. The Cascada de la Virgen, a gentle waterfall surrounded by lush vegetation, offers a tranquil setting where visitors can pause and soak in the beauty of their surroundings. Smaller tributaries and hidden corners of the river provide moments of solitude, where the interplay of light and water creates constantly shifting patterns that feel like nature's own art.

Walking along the riverbanks, you can't help but notice the intricate details that make up this ecosystem. The rocks, sculpted by centuries of flowing water, are covered in patterns and textures that tell the story of the river's geological history. Tiny fish dart through the clear waters, their movements adding life to the underwater landscape. Dragonflies hover above the surface, their iridescent wings catching the sunlight. Every element of the river, from the smallest insect to the towering trees that line its banks, contributes to the delicate balance that sustains this vibrant environment.

The Serranía de la Macarena, the mountain range that cradles Caño Cristales, is itself a place of immense ecological significance. This region is a meeting point for three major ecosystems: the Amazon rainforest, the Andes Mountains, and the Orinoco plains. This convergence has created a biodiversity hotspot, home to an astonishing variety of plant and animal species. Jaguars, capybaras, and tapirs roam the forests, while the skies are filled with the calls of toucans, parrots, and harpy eagles. The region's flora is equally diverse, ranging from towering ceiba trees to delicate orchids that bloom in the shade of the forest canopy.

The human history of the region is as rich as its natural heritage. The indigenous communities who have called this area home for centuries possess a deep understanding of its landscapes and ecosystems. Their knowledge, passed down through generations, has been instrumental in preserving the delicate balance of the region. Many of these communities are actively involved in conservation efforts, working alongside scientists and environmental organizations to protect Caño Cristales and its surroundings. Their stories and traditions add a layer of cultural depth to the experience, reminding visitors that this is not just a place of beauty but also one of profound connection between people and the land.

Sustainability is at the heart of any visit to Caño Cristales. The Colombian government and local authorities have implemented strict regulations to protect the river and its fragile ecosystem. Visitor numbers are limited, and all tours must be conducted with licensed guides to ensure that the area is treated with the utmost respect. Swimming is permitted in designated areas only, and visitors are prohibited from using sunscreen or insect repellent that could harm the aquatic plants. These measures are a testament to the commitment of local communities and officials to preserving this natural wonder for future generations.

The experience of Caño Cristales is deeply personal, a journey that resonates differently for each visitor. For some, it is a place of wonder and discovery, a chance to witness one of nature's most extraordinary spectacles. For others, it is a place of reflection, where the beauty and fragility of the river evoke a sense of awe and responsibility. Standing on the banks of Caño Cristales, it is impossible not to feel a connection to the broader web of life, a reminder of the intricate relationships that sustain our planet.

As evening falls and the colors of the river begin to fade with the setting sun, the journey back to La Macarena offers a moment to absorb the day's experiences. The quiet hum of the boat's motor, the gentle lapping of water against its sides, and the silhouettes of trees against the fading light create a sense of calm and gratitude. Caño Cristales is not just a destination;

it is a testament to the beauty and resilience of nature, a place that inspires both wonder and responsibility. Its colors may fade with the seasons, but its impact lingers, a vivid reminder of the treasures that await those who venture off the beaten path.

# Los Nevados National Park: Hiking in the Andes

Los Nevados National Park, located in the heart of Colombia's central Andes, is a breathtaking expanse of dramatic peaks, glacial lakes, páramo ecosystems, and volcanic landscapes. Spanning over 583 square kilometers across the departments of Caldas, Risaralda, Quindío, and Tolima, the park is one of the most significant natural reserves in the country. It is home to towering volcanoes like Nevado del Ruiz, Nevado de Santa Isabel, and Nevado del Tolima, each offering unique challenges and unparalleled vistas for hikers and adventurers. The park's diverse ecosystems, ranging from lush cloud forests to the high-altitude páramo, make it a place of extraordinary ecological and geological value. Hiking through this remarkable region is not only a physical journey but also a deeply immersive experience in one of the most pristine and awe-inspiring corners of Colombia.

The first step to exploring Los Nevados begins with preparation, as its diverse terrain requires a well-thought-out plan. The park's altitude ranges from 2,600 meters to over 5,300 meters above sea level, meaning visitors will encounter a variety of climates and conditions during their trek. Packing appropriately is crucial: layers of clothing to adapt to the temperature shifts, sturdy waterproof boots for uneven trails, and essentials like sunscreen, a hat, and gloves to protect against the fierce sun and cold winds at higher altitudes. Acclimatization to the altitude is just as vital, as the thin air at these elevations can pose challenges for those unaccustomed to it. Spending a day or two in nearby towns like Manizales or Pereira, which sit at moderate elevations, can help hikers prepare their bodies for the rigors ahead.

The gateway to the park often depends on the specific trail or summit visitors wish to explore. Manizales serves as a common entry point for those seeking access to Nevado del Ruiz, the park's most famous peak, while Salento and Pereira are ideal bases for those aiming to explore the verdant Cocora Valley and embark on longer treks toward Nevado del Tolima. Each town offers local guides and tour operators who are not only knowledgeable about the park's geography but also deeply familiar with its delicate ecosystems and cultural significance. Hiring a guide is highly recommended, particularly for those attempting more challenging routes or summits, as they provide invaluable expertise and ensure safety in this rugged, unpredictable environment.

Hiking in Los Nevados often begins with a journey through the páramo, a unique high-altitude ecosystem found only in certain parts of the Andes. The páramo is a surreal landscape of rolling grasslands, towering frailejones, and mist-shrouded valleys. Frailejones, with their spiky, silvery leaves and thick stalks, dominate the terrain, giving the impression of an alien world. These plants are not only visually striking but also vital to the ecosystem, as they capture and store water, feeding the streams and rivers that sustain life in the region. Walking through the páramo is both humbling and enchanting, as the stillness of the landscape is broken only by the occasional call of a highland bird or the rustle of the wind through the grasses.

For many, the main draw of Los Nevados is the chance to ascend one of its majestic volcanic peaks. Nevado del Ruiz, standing at 5,321 meters, is the most accessible of the park's summits and a popular choice for those seeking a challenging but achievable climb. Despite its beauty, Nevado del Ruiz is an active stratovolcano, and its history includes several eruptions, the most devastating of which occurred in 1985 and caused the tragic Armero disaster. Today, climbing the volcano is closely monitored, with access restricted to ensure the safety of visitors. Reaching the glacier line on Nevado del Ruiz is an unforgettable experience, where the icy expanse of the glacier contrasts starkly with the dark volcanic rock and the endless sky above. The effort required to climb to this altitude is rewarded with panoramic views that stretch across the Andes, a sight that stays etched in the memory long after the descent.

For those seeking a more remote and challenging adventure, Nevado del Tolima offers an entirely different experience. This volcano, rising to 5,276 meters, is less accessible than Nevado del Ruiz and requires a multi-day trek through some of the park's most rugged terrain. The journey begins in the lush forests of the Cocora Valley, where towering wax palms—the tallest palm trees in the world—stand sentinel over the trail. As the path climbs higher, the landscape gradually transitions from cloud forest to páramo, with the vegetation becoming sparser and the air thinner. The final ascent to the summit of Nevado del Tolima is a test of endurance and determination, but those who reach the top are rewarded with a sense of accomplishment and a view that few others have experienced.

Nevado de Santa Isabel, at 4,965 meters, offers a gentler alternative for hikers who wish to experience the beauty of the park without the extreme challenges posed by its taller peaks. This glacier-capped volcano is known for its accessibility and relatively moderate trails, making it a popular choice for beginner mountaineers or those with limited time. The trek to Santa Isabel's glacier is a journey through a landscape of otherworldly beauty, where the contrast between the white ice, the dark volcanic rock, and the vibrant greens of the páramo creates a stunning visual tableau. The glacier itself is a sobering reminder of the effects of climate change, as it has receded significantly in recent decades, underscoring the importance of preserving these fragile environments.

Beyond its volcanic peaks, Los Nevados is home to a network of glacial lakes that add another layer of beauty to the park's landscape. Laguna Otún, one of the most famous, is a shimmering body of water surrounded by rugged cliffs and páramo vegetation. The lake, fed by glacial meltwater, is a serene spot that offers a moment of reflection amidst the challenges of the hike. Other lakes, like Laguna Verde and Laguna del Encanto, are equally captivating, their still waters reflecting the sky and surrounding peaks like natural mirrors. These lakes are not only scenic highlights but also vital habitats for the park's wildlife, including Andean ducks and other bird species.

Wildlife in Los Nevados is as diverse as its landscapes, with the park serving as a refuge for several iconic Andean species. The Andean condor, with its impressive wingspan, can occasionally be seen soaring above the peaks, a symbol of the park's untamed beauty. Other species, such as spectacled bears, páramo deer, and mountain tapirs, inhabit the park's more remote areas, though sightings are rare and considered a privilege. Birdwatchers will find the park particularly rewarding, as it is home to a variety of endemic and migratory bird species, from hummingbirds to tanagers.

The experience of hiking in Los Nevados is not only about the physical journey but also about connecting with the natural and cultural heritage of the Andes. The park's landscapes are deeply intertwined with the history and traditions of the local communities, many of whom have lived in harmony with this environment for generations. These communities, including indigenous peoples and highland farmers, play a crucial role in preserving the park's ecosystems and cultural significance. Visitors have the opportunity to learn about their way of life, from traditional farming practices to the spiritual significance of the mountains, adding depth and meaning to the hiking experience.

Leaving Los Nevados National Park is a bittersweet moment, as the memories of its towering peaks, serene páramos, and glistening glaciers linger long after the journey ends. It is a place that challenges the body, inspires the soul, and fosters a deep appreciation for the natural wonders of the Andes. For those who venture into its rugged terrain, Los Nevados offers not just a hike but an unforgettable encounter with the raw beauty and resilience of Colombia's highlands. It is a reminder of the power of nature and the importance of preserving it for future generations.

# San Andrés and Providencia: Colombia's Island Paradise

San Andrés and Providencia, a stunning archipelago in the Caribbean Sea, are often regarded as Colombia's island paradise. Located about 775 kilometers northwest of mainland Colombia, these islands are a blend of pristine beaches, vibrant culture, and a unique ecosystem that sets them apart from other tropical destinations. The turquoise waters surrounding the islands are famous for their "sea of seven colors," a phenomenon caused by varying depths, sunlight, and coral reefs that create a mosaic of blues and greens. Beyond their natural beauty, San Andrés and Providencia are steeped in history and tradition, offering visitors a chance to explore not only their breathtaking landscapes but also the rich cultural heritage of the Raizal community, whose Afro-Caribbean roots define much of the islands' identity.

San Andrés, the larger and more developed of the two islands, is the starting point for most visitors. Its main town is bustling with activity, offering everything from lively markets to duty-free shopping, as the island is a designated free-trade zone. Despite its commercial side, San Andrés retains a laid-back island vibe, with reggae music wafting through the air and locals greeting visitors with warm smiles. The island's compact size makes it easy to explore, whether by rented golf cart, scooter, or bicycle, all of which allow for a leisurely pace and the chance to take in the scenery at every turn.

One of San Andrés' most iconic attractions is Johnny Cay, a small islet just a short boat ride from the main island. This lush, palm-covered oasis is surrounded by powdery white sand and crystal-clear waters, making it an ideal spot for swimming, snorkeling, or simply relaxing under the shade of a coconut tree. The waters around Johnny Cay teem with marine life, offering snorkelers the chance to see colorful fish darting among the coral. The islet's beach bars serve up fresh seafood, tropical cocktails, and coconut rice, giving visitors a taste of the Caribbean's culinary delights.

Another must-visit site on San Andrés is the Hoyo Soplador, a natural blowhole located on the southern tip of the island. This geological wonder is created by waves forcing air and water through an underwater tunnel, shooting a powerful spray into the air. Visitors often gather around the blowhole, waiting for the next burst of seawater while enjoying the dramatic views of the coastline. Nearby, the beaches of San Luis provide a quieter alternative to the busier areas of the island. Lined with wooden houses painted in bright colors, San Luis exudes old-world charm and offers a more relaxed atmosphere for sunbathing and swimming.

For those interested in exploring San Andrés' underwater world, the island offers some of the best diving and snorkeling opportunities in the Caribbean. The coral reefs surrounding the island are part of the Seaflower Biosphere Reserve, a UNESCO-designated area that protects one of the most important marine ecosystems in the region. Dive sites such as El Acuario and La Piscinita are renowned for their visibility, diverse marine life, and vibrant coral formations. Beginners and experienced divers alike can marvel at the underwater landscapes, which include shipwrecks, underwater caves, and schools of tropical fish. The shallow, calm waters also make these sites ideal for snorkeling, allowing even novice swimmers to experience the magic beneath the waves.

Providencia, located about 90 kilometers north of San Andrés, offers a stark contrast to its larger neighbor. This smaller, less developed island is a haven of tranquility, where time seems to slow down and nature takes center stage. Providencia is reached by a short flight or ferry ride from San Andrés, and the journey itself feels like stepping back in time. The island's rugged beauty, with its lush hills, pristine beaches, and unspoiled coral reefs, creates an atmosphere of serenity and seclusion that appeals to travelers seeking an escape from the modern world.

One of Providencia's most remarkable features is its proximity to the third-largest barrier reef in the world. This reef system, which stretches for miles, is a treasure trove of biodiversity, home to hundreds of species of coral, fish, and other marine life. Diving and snorkeling here are unparalleled experiences, offering encounters with nurse sharks, rays, and sea turtles in a setting that feels untouched by human impact. The waters around Providencia are also ideal for kayaking and paddleboarding, allowing visitors to explore the mangroves and hidden coves that dot the coastline.

The centerpiece of Providencia's natural beauty is Crab Cay, a tiny islet located just off the island's eastern shore. Accessible by boat, Crab Cay is part of the McBean Lagoon National Natural Park and is a must-visit for anyone exploring Providencia. The cay's crystal-clear waters are perfect for snorkeling, with vibrant coral reefs just a short swim from the shore. Climbing to the top of the cay offers panoramic views of the surrounding sea, where the "seven colors" phenomenon is even more pronounced. The interplay of light and water creates a kaleidoscope of blues and greens, a sight that leaves visitors in awe of nature's artistry.

Providencia's charm extends beyond its natural beauty to its cultural heritage, which is deeply rooted in the traditions of the Raizal people. This Afro-Caribbean community has preserved its unique language, music, and customs, creating a cultural identity that is distinct from mainland Colombia. The Raizal language, a Creole dialect with influences from English, Spanish, and African languages, is widely spoken on the island and adds to its sense of authenticity. Visitors are often struck by the warmth and hospitality of the Raizal people, who take pride in sharing their culture with others.

Traditional Raizal cuisine is another highlight of the Providencia experience. Seafood plays a central role in the local diet, with dishes like rondón—a hearty stew made with fish, coconut milk, cassava, and plantains—showcasing the island's culinary prowess. Freshly caught lobster, grilled to perfection and served with coconut rice, is a staple of many beachfront restaurants. The flavors of Providencia are a reflection of its history and geography, blending Caribbean and Colombian influences into dishes that are as vibrant as the island itself.

One of Providencia's cultural landmarks is the bridge that connects it to Santa Catalina, a smaller island just off its northern coast. Known as the Lovers' Bridge, this wooden structure spans the narrow channel between the two islands, offering stunning views of the turquoise waters below. Santa Catalina is a quiet retreat, with no cars and only a handful of residents, making it an ideal place for a peaceful stroll or a day of relaxation. The island is also home to Fort Warwick, a historic site that dates back to the colonial era and offers a glimpse into Providencia's storied past.

The natural and cultural treasures of San Andrés and Providencia are not without challenges. The archipelago faces threats from climate change, overfishing, and unsustainable tourism practices, all of which have the potential to disrupt its delicate ecosystems and way of life. Efforts are being made to promote responsible tourism, with initiatives that emphasize conservation and community involvement. Visitors to the islands are encouraged to respect the environment, support local businesses, and learn about the Raizal culture, ensuring that their presence contributes positively to the region.

San Andrés and Providencia are more than just idyllic islands; they are living, breathing communities with a rich history and a deep connection to their natural surroundings. Exploring their beaches, reefs, and villages is an experience that goes beyond sightseeing, offering a chance to engage with the people and landscapes that make this corner of the Caribbean so special. Whether you're diving into the "sea of seven colors," savoring a plate of rondón, or simply watching the sunset from a quiet beach, these islands leave a lasting impression that stays with you long after you've departed. They are a reminder of the beauty and resilience of nature and the importance of preserving it for generations to come.

# Chicamocha Canyon: Colombia's Grand Canyon

Carved over millions of years by the relentless flow of the Chicamocha River, Chicamocha Canyon stands as one of

Colombia's most awe-inspiring natural wonders. Stretching across the Santander Department in northeastern Colombia, this massive canyon is often compared to the Grand Canyon in the United States, though it has its own unique character and charm. With its dramatic cliffs, winding river, and panoramic vistas, Chicamocha Canyon is not only a geological marvel but also a playground for adventurers, nature lovers, and those seeking a deeper connection to Colombia's raw beauty. Its vastness and rugged terrain have become a symbol of the region's resilience and strength, drawing visitors eager to explore its breathtaking landscapes and rich cultural heritage.

The first glimpse of Chicamocha Canyon is nothing short of breathtaking. As you approach from the surrounding towns, the land suddenly opens up to reveal a vast chasm that seems to stretch endlessly into the horizon. The canyon's steep walls, adorned with layers of sedimentary rock in earthy tones of red, orange, and brown, bear witness to the passage of time and the forces of nature that shaped this extraordinary place. The Chicamocha River snakes through the bottom of the canyon, its waters glinting in the sunlight as it carves its way through the rugged terrain. The scale of the canyon is humbling, a reminder of the immense power of geological processes and the beauty they create.

One of the best ways to experience the grandeur of Chicamocha Canyon is to visit Chicamocha National Park, or Panachi, a sprawling complex perched on a ridge that offers unparalleled views of the canyon. The park is a hub of activity, blending adventure, education, and culture into a single destination. Visitors can take advantage of the park's cable car system, one of the longest in the world, which descends nearly 1,350 meters into the canyon before climbing back up the other side. The ride offers a bird's-eye view of the canyon's sheer cliffs and winding river, a perspective that highlights its immense scale and beauty. The cable car is not just a mode of transportation—it's an experience that encapsulates the essence of Chicamocha Canyon.

For those seeking an adrenaline rush, Chicamocha Canyon offers a host of adventure activities that take full advantage of its rugged terrain. Paragliding is one of the most popular options, allowing thrill-seekers to soar above the canyon and take in its vastness from the sky. The feeling of gliding through the air, with the wind rushing past and the canyon spread out below, is exhilarating and unforgettable. Hiking is another way to connect with the canyon's landscapes, with trails ranging from leisurely walks to challenging treks that lead to remote viewpoints and hidden corners. The rocky terrain, steep inclines, and sweeping vistas make every step an adventure, rewarding hikers with a deeper appreciation of the canyon's raw beauty.

Mountain biking is a thrilling way to explore Chicamocha Canyon for those who prefer wheels over wings or walking boots. The rugged trails that wind through the canyon provide a perfect setting for this high-energy activity, with sharp descents, tight turns, and spectacular scenery at every twist and turn. Riders navigate paths that cut through the arid landscape, passing cacti, scrub vegetation, and the occasional grazing goat. The combination of physical exertion and stunning surroundings creates an experience that is as challenging as it is rewarding. The canyon's dry climate and rocky terrain make it essential to come prepared, with plenty of water, sun protection, and a sturdy bike suited for off-road conditions.

Beyond its natural beauty, Chicamocha Canyon is steeped in cultural significance, particularly for the Guane people, an indigenous group that once inhabited the region. The Guane left behind a legacy that can still be seen today in the form of petroglyphs, pottery, and other artifacts that offer a glimpse into their way of life. The nearby town of Barichara, often referred to as the most beautiful town in Colombia, is a testament to the enduring influence of the Guane culture. Its cobblestone streets, whitewashed buildings, and terracotta roofs reflect the region's colonial history, while its artisans and craftspeople keep traditional techniques alive. Visiting Barichara is like stepping back in time, a chance to connect with the region's past while enjoying its serene charm.

Another cultural gem near Chicamocha Canyon is the Camino Real, an ancient stone pathway that links Barichara to the village of Guane. This historic trail, originally built by the indigenous Guane people and later expanded during the colonial era, is a popular route for hikers seeking a mix of natural beauty and cultural heritage. The trail winds through rolling hills and arid landscapes, offering stunning views of the canyon and the surrounding countryside. Along the way, hikers encounter small farms, grazing livestock, and the occasional local eager to share stories of the region's history and traditions. The Camino Real is more than just a path; it is a living connection to the people and places that define this part of Colombia.

The flora and fauna of Chicamocha Canyon add another layer of richness to its allure. The canyon's arid climate supports a unique ecosystem characterized by cacti, agave plants, and other hardy vegetation adapted to the harsh conditions. Birds are particularly abundant, with species such as the Andean condor, hawks, and colorful tanagers frequently spotted soaring above the canyon or perched on rocky outcrops. The biodiversity of the region is a reminder of nature's adaptability and resilience, qualities that resonate deeply in a place as rugged and untamed as Chicamocha.

One of the most rewarding experiences in Chicamocha Canyon is simply taking a moment to sit and absorb its vastness. Whether perched on a rocky ledge or standing at a viewpoint in the national park, the sheer scale of the canyon inspires a sense of awe and introspection. The play of light and shadow across the canyon walls as the sun moves through the sky creates a constantly shifting palette of colors and textures. Sunrise and sunset are particularly magical times, when the canyon is bathed in golden light and the surrounding landscape takes on a dreamlike quality. These moments of stillness and beauty are a reminder of the power of nature to evoke wonder and connection.

Chicamocha Canyon is not without its challenges. The region's arid climate and rugged terrain can be demanding, particularly for those unaccustomed to such conditions. It is essential to come prepared, with plenty of water, sun protection, and appropriate footwear for hiking or exploring. Additionally, the canyon's fragile ecosystems require careful stewardship to ensure that they remain intact for future generations. Visitors are encouraged to tread lightly, respect local regulations, and support sustainable tourism initiatives that benefit both the environment and the local communities.

For many, Chicamocha Canyon is more than just a destination—it is a journey into the heart of Colombia's natural and cultural heritage. Its towering cliffs and winding river tell a story of geological transformation, while its trails and towns preserve the memory of the people who have called this region home for centuries. Exploring Chicamocha Canyon is an opportunity to connect with something larger than oneself, to feel the timeless pull of the earth and the enduring spirit of its landscapes. It is a place that challenges, inspires, and leaves a lasting impression, a reminder of the beauty and resilience of the natural world.

# CHAPTER 3: COLOMBIA'S RICH HISTORY AND CULTURE

## Pre-Colombian Civilizations: From the Muisca to the Tairona

Pre-Colombian civilizations in Colombia laid the foundations of a rich cultural heritage that continues to echo through the country's landscapes, traditions, and artifacts. Long before Spanish explorers set foot on these lands, advanced societies like the Muisca, Tairona, Quimbaya, and San Agustín thrived, creating sophisticated systems of governance, religion, and art. These civilizations flourished in different regions, each adapting to the unique landscapes of mountains, valleys, and coasts. Their legacies—preserved in gold artifacts, stone carvings, and oral traditions—offer glimpses into a world that was once vibrant, complex, and deeply interconnected with nature. The stories of the Muisca and Tairona peoples, in particular, stand out as testaments to the ingenuity and resilience of these ancient cultures.

The Muisca civilization, one of the most prominent pre-Colombian cultures in Colombia, inhabited the high-altitude plateaus of the Eastern Andes. These fertile lands, known as the Altiplano Cundiboyacense, provided the Muisca with an ideal environment for agriculture and settlement. The Muisca were part of the larger Chibcha linguistic family and were known for their highly organized society, which was divided into two main confederations: Bacatá (modern-day Bogotá) and Hunza (modern-day Tunja). Each confederation was ruled by a leader, known as a zipa in Bacatá and a zaque in Hunza, with these leaders wielding significant political and religious power. The Muisca created a system of governance that was both hierarchical and collaborative, with smaller local rulers, or caciques, answering to the zipa and zaque.

Central to Muisca culture was their mastery of agriculture. The Muisca people cultivated crops such as maize, potatoes, quinoa, and cotton, using advanced techniques like terracing and irrigation to maximize productivity in their mountainous environment. They also developed an intricate system of trade, exchanging goods like salt, emeralds, and gold with neighboring tribes and regions. Salt, in particular, was a highly prized commodity, extracted from natural salt mines in areas like Zipaquirá and Nemocón using evaporation techniques. This "white gold" was not only a vital resource for preserving food but also a key element in the Muisca's economic and cultural exchanges.

The Muisca are perhaps best known for their remarkable goldwork, which reflected their spiritual beliefs and artistic prowess. Gold held a sacred significance for the Muisca, symbolizing the energy of the sun and serving as a medium for communicating with their gods. Their most famous artifact is the Muisca raft, or "Balsa Muisca," a small golden figure depicting a ceremonial scene involving the legendary El Dorado ritual. The raft portrays a chieftain adorned with gold, standing on a boat surrounded by priests and offerings. This ritual, performed at Lake Guatavita, involved the leader covering himself in gold dust and casting treasures into the lake as offerings to the gods. Though the legend of El Dorado became a driving force for Spanish conquistadors seeking unimaginable wealth, for the Muisca, it was a deeply spiritual ceremony rooted in their cosmology.

Religion played a central role in Muisca society, with their deities closely tied to natural elements and celestial bodies. Bochica, the god of civilization and wisdom, was a revered figure who, according to legend, taught the Muisca people agriculture, law, and morality. Chía, the moon goddess, and Sué, the sun god, were also significant, representing the duality and balance of life. Muisca temples, often constructed on high ground to be closer to the heavens, served as centers of worship and community gatherings. The remains of these sacred sites, such as those at the archaeological park of Facatativá, offer insights into the spiritual practices of this remarkable civilization.

While the Muisca thrived in the Andes, the Tairona civilization flourished in the lush foothills of the Sierra Nevada de Santa Marta along Colombia's northern coast. The Tairona were a highly organized society known for their impressive urban planning, agricultural ingenuity, and stunning craftsmanship. Their settlements were strategically located in the mountains, with terraced fields, stone pathways, and drainage systems that reflected their deep understanding of the natural environment. The most famous of these sites is Ciudad Perdida, or the Lost City, a sprawling archaeological complex thought to have been a major ceremonial and administrative center.

Ciudad Perdida, or Teyuna as it is known in indigenous lore, is a testament to the architectural and engineering skills of the Tairona people. The site features circular stone terraces, plazas, and staircases that blend seamlessly with the surrounding jungle. Reaching Ciudad Perdida requires a challenging trek through dense rainforest, steep inclines, and river crossings, a journey that mirrors the isolation and mystique of the ancient city. The Tairona's ability to construct such an intricate settlement in the heart of the jungle speaks to their resourcefulness and their harmonious relationship with nature. The city was abandoned during the Spanish conquest, but it remains a sacred site for the Kogi, Wiwa, and Arhuaco peoples, who are descendants of the Tairona and continue to honor their ancestors' legacy.

Like the Muisca, the Tairona were skilled artisans, particularly in the creation of gold and tumbaga (a gold-copper alloy) artifacts. Their jewelry and ceremonial objects, often shaped into intricate designs of animals, plants, and spiritual symbols, demonstrate a profound connection to their environment and beliefs. The Tairona also excelled in pottery and weaving, producing goods that were both functional and artistic. These crafts were not merely decorative; they were imbued with spiritual significance, serving as offerings, status symbols, and expressions of identity.

The Tairona's relationship with the natural world extended to their agricultural practices, which were adapted to the challenging terrain of the Sierra Nevada. They utilized terracing to create fertile fields on steep slopes, cultivating crops such as maize, beans, and cassava. Their knowledge of the land allowed them to maintain a sustainable lifestyle, ensuring the long-term health of their environment. This balance between human activity and nature remains a cornerstone of the traditional practices of their descendants, who continue to advocate for the preservation of the Sierra Nevada as a sacred and ecological sanctuary.

Both the Muisca and Tairona civilizations offer invaluable insights into the ingenuity and spirituality of pre-Colombian societies in Colombia. While they faced different geographical and environmental challenges, their shared ability to adapt, innovate, and thrive in harmony with their surroundings is a testament to their resilience and wisdom. The artifacts, ruins, and oral traditions they left behind are not just remnants of the past—they are living reminders of the deep connections between culture, nature, and identity.

The arrival of Spanish conquistadors in the 16th century marked a dramatic turning point for the Muisca, Tairona, and other indigenous groups across Colombia. Many of their societies were disrupted or destroyed, their populations decimated by disease, conflict, and forced assimilation. However, their legacies endure in the landscapes they shaped, the artifacts they crafted, and the traditions carried on by their descendants. Today, efforts to preserve and honor these pre-Colombian cultures are gaining momentum, with archaeologists, historians, and indigenous communities working together to protect their heritage and share their stories with the world.

Exploring the history of the Muisca and Tairona civilizations is more than an academic exercise—it is an opportunity to understand the roots of Colombia's identity and the enduring influence of its indigenous peoples. Their achievements in art, agriculture, and governance continue to inspire, offering lessons in sustainability, resilience, and the importance of living in harmony with the natural world. For those who walk the paths of Ciudad Perdida, visit the salt mines of Zipaquirá, or marvel at the gold artifacts in Bogotá's Museo del Oro, the past comes alive in vivid detail, a reminder of the profound contributions of these ancient civilizations to Colombia's cultural tapestry.

## The Spanish Conquest and Colonial Era

The Spanish conquest of Colombia, beginning in the early 16th century, marked one of the most transformative and tumultuous chapters in the country's history. With the arrival of Spanish explorers and later settlers, the lives of the indigenous peoples who had thrived for centuries were irreversibly changed. The conquest brought both devastation and new cultural dynamics that would shape the foundation of modern Colombia. The colonial era that followed saw the emergence of a society defined by a complex interplay of power, religion, exploitation, and cultural blending. Understanding this period is essential to comprehending the roots of Colombia's identity and the legacies that continue to influence its contemporary landscape.

The first Spanish expeditions into what is now Colombia were driven by the search for wealth and conquest. In 1499, Alonso de Ojeda, an explorer who had sailed with Christopher Columbus, reached the northern shores of South America, planting the seeds of European interest in the region. Over the following decades, expeditions pushed inland, lured by tales of gold and prosperous civilizations. One of the most enduring legends that fueled these ventures was that of El Dorado, a mythical city of gold. This story, linked to the Muisca civilization, captivated the imaginations of Spanish conquistadors and led them deep into the Andes in search of unimaginable riches.

The arrival of Gonzalo Jiménez de Quesada in 1536 marked the beginning of a more concerted effort to establish Spanish control in Colombia. Leading an expedition up the Magdalena River, Quesada and his men endured treacherous conditions, disease, and hostile terrain as they made their way toward the highlands. By the time they reached the Muisca heartland in the Altiplano Cundiboyacense, their numbers had dwindled, but they still managed to subdue the indigenous population through a combination of military force, deceit, and the spread of European diseases to which the Muisca had no immunity. The conquest of the Muisca Confederation, with its wealth of gold and salt, was a significant achievement for the Spanish and laid the groundwork for the establishment of Bogotá in 1538, which became the nucleus of colonial rule in the region.

The conquest was not limited to the Muisca. Other powerful indigenous groups, such as the Tairona in the Sierra Nevada de Santa Marta and the Quimbaya in the coffee-growing regions of the west, also faced the onslaught of Spanish forces. The Tairona, known for their advanced urban planning and gold craftsmanship, resisted fiercely but were eventually decimated by a combination of violence and disease. The Quimbaya, whose intricate gold artifacts remain some of the most celebrated examples of pre-Colombian art, suffered a similar fate. The Spanish imposed their authority through brutality and exploitation, dismantling indigenous societies and seizing control of their lands and resources.

As Spanish dominance solidified, the colonial era began, characterized by the establishment of the Viceroyalty of New Granada in 1717. This administrative division, which included present-day Colombia, Ecuador, Panama, and Venezuela, was created to better manage the Spanish Empire's American territories. Bogotá became a key center of governance, and the colonial administration worked to impose Spanish laws, religion, and culture on the indigenous population. The Catholic Church played a central role in this process, acting as both a spiritual and political force. Missionaries and clergy were tasked with converting indigenous peoples to Christianity, often by force, and reshaping their cultural practices to align with European ideals.

The spread of Catholicism was accompanied by the construction of churches, monasteries, and schools, many of which still stand today as architectural testaments to the colonial period. The city of Popayán, for instance, became a center of religious activity, known for its grand churches and Semana Santa (Holy Week) processions. However, the imposition of Christianity often involved the suppression of indigenous spiritual beliefs and practices, leading to a loss of cultural heritage. Despite this, many indigenous communities found ways to preserve elements of their traditions, blending them with Catholic rituals in a process known as syncretism.

The economic structure of colonial Colombia was built on the exploitation of both land and labor. Encomiendas, a system in which Spanish settlers were granted control over indigenous communities in exchange for their labor and tribute, became the primary means of extracting wealth from the land. This system, which was justified by the Crown as a way to protect and Christianize indigenous peoples, in reality subjected them to harsh conditions and exploitation. Over time, as the indigenous population declined due to disease and overwork, African slaves were brought to Colombia to work in mines, plantations, and other labor-intensive industries. The transatlantic slave trade introduced a new layer of cultural and demographic complexity to the region, as African traditions and practices became part of the colonial fabric.

Gold mining was one of the most important economic activities during the colonial period, with Colombia becoming one of the Spanish Empire's primary sources of the precious metal. Towns such as Santa Fé de Antioquia and Zaragoza grew around mining operations, attracting settlers and laborers. The extraction of gold not only fueled the empire's wealth but also reinforced the social hierarchies that defined colonial society. At the top were the peninsulares, Spaniards born in Europe, followed by criollos, or Spaniards born in the Americas. Below them were mestizos, people of mixed European and indigenous heritage, and at the bottom of the social ladder were indigenous peoples and African slaves. This rigid caste system shaped every aspect of colonial life, from politics to daily interactions.

Agriculture also played a crucial role in the colonial economy, with crops such as sugarcane, tobacco, and cacao cultivated on large estates known as haciendas. These estates were often worked by enslaved Africans and indigenous laborers, whose lives were marked by hardship and oppression. The hacienda system not only concentrated wealth and power in the hands of a few elite families but also contributed to the widespread inequality that continues to affect Colombia today. Despite the harsh conditions, enslaved and marginalized communities found ways to resist and assert their humanity, preserving their cultural identities and forging new ones in the face of adversity.

By the late 18th century, the colonial order began to show signs of strain. Economic restrictions imposed by the Spanish Crown, combined with growing discontent among the criollo elite, created an environment ripe for change. Enlightenment ideas of liberty, equality, and self-determination began to spread throughout the Americas, inspiring movements for independence. In Colombia, the seeds of revolution were sown in cities like Bogotá and Cartagena, where intellectuals, merchants, and military leaders began to challenge the colonial status quo.

The legacy of the Spanish conquest and colonial era is both profound and complex. While it brought devastating consequences for indigenous populations and entrenched systems of exploitation, it also laid the groundwork for the cultural and social diversity that defines Colombia today. The blending of European, indigenous, and African influences has created a rich tapestry of traditions, languages, and identities that continue to evolve. The gold artifacts of the Muisca, the stone carvings of the San Agustín culture, and the vibrant rhythms of Afro-Colombian music are all testaments to the resilience and creativity of the peoples who have shaped this land.

Understanding this history is essential for appreciating the depth and complexity of Colombia's cultural heritage. It is a story of conquest and resistance, of destruction and creation, and of the enduring human spirit in the face of profound change. The echoes of the colonial era can still be felt in Colombia's cities and landscapes, reminding us of the forces that have shaped this nation and the resilience of its people in forging a future from the shadows of its past.

# Independence and the Birth of Modern Colombia

The fight for independence in Colombia was a turbulent and transformative period that reshaped the nation, marking the end of Spanish colonial rule and the beginning of the country's journey toward modernity. The process was neither swift nor easy, marked by conflict, betrayal, and sacrifice. Yet, it was also a time of immense hope and determination, driven by the ideals of liberty and self-determination. The birth of modern Colombia was forged in the crucible of revolution, with key historical events and figures paving the way for the establishment of a republic. Understanding this pivotal era in Colombian history reveals the roots of the nation's identity and the struggles that continue to shape its development.

By the late 18th century, the Spanish colonies in the Americas were growing restless under the weight of imperial restrictions. The Bourbon Reforms, introduced by the Spanish Crown to centralize authority and increase revenue, placed significant economic and political pressures on the colonies. Trade restrictions, increased taxes, and the exclusion of local criollos—individuals of Spanish descent born in the Americas—from key administrative positions created widespread resentment. Enlightenment ideas, which emphasized reason, equality, and the rights of individuals, began to take hold among the educated elite, further fueling discontent. These ideological shifts, combined with inspiration from the American and French revolutions, set the stage for revolutionary movements across Latin America, including Colombia.

The movement for Colombian independence gained momentum in the early 19th century. One of the earliest sparks occurred on July 20, 1810, in Bogotá, when tensions between criollos and peninsulares—Spaniards born in Europe—erupted into open defiance. The event, known as the Florero de Llorente incident, unfolded at a local shop where an argument over a borrowed flower vase escalated into a public confrontation. Though the disagreement itself was trivial, it became a catalyst for broader grievances against colonial rule. That same day, criollo leaders seized the opportunity to convene a cabildo abierto, or open council, declaring a provisional government and marking the beginning of Colombia's independence movement.

Despite the initial enthusiasm, the path to independence was fraught with challenges. The early years of the movement, known as the Patria Boba or "Foolish Fatherland," were characterized by internal divisions among the revolutionaries. Criollo leaders disagreed on the structure of government, the extent of autonomy from Spain, and the inclusion of other social groups in the fight for independence. Regional rivalries further complicated efforts to build a unified front, with cities like Bogotá, Cartagena, and Popayán vying for influence. These disagreements weakened the movement and allowed Spanish loyalists, or royalists, to regain control of many territories by 1816, with brutal reprisals against those who had supported the revolution.

Amid this turmoil, one figure emerged as a unifying force and a symbol of the independence struggle: Simón Bolívar. Born in Caracas, Bolívar was a charismatic military leader and visionary who dedicated his life to liberating South America from Spanish rule. His campaign to free Colombia began in earnest in 1819, with a daring plan to cross the Andes and launch a surprise attack on the royalist forces stationed in New Granada. The journey was grueling, with Bolívar's army enduring freezing temperatures, treacherous terrain, and dwindling supplies. Yet, their perseverance paid off with a decisive victory at the Battle of Boyacá on August 7, 1819. This triumph marked a turning point in the war, leading to the liberation of Bogotá and the establishment of the Republic of Colombia, also known as Gran Colombia.

Gran Colombia was an ambitious political project that united the territories of present day Colombia, Venezuela, Ecuador, and Panama under a single government. Bolívar envisioned a federation of independent states, inspired by the ideals of liberty and unity. However, the republic faced significant challenges from the outset. Regional differences, economic disparities, and competing political ideologies created tensions within the newly formed nation. Bolívar's dream of a united South America ultimately proved unsustainable, and Gran Colombia dissolved in 1831, with the territories splitting into separate nations. Despite its short-lived existence, Gran Colombia laid the foundation for the modern Colombian state and cemented Bolívar's legacy as the Liberator.

The years following independence were marked by political instability and the struggle to define Colombia's identity as a republic. The abolition of colonial structures left a power vacuum, with competing factions vying for control. Two dominant political ideologies emerged during this period: centralism, which advocated for a strong, centralized government, and federalism, which favored greater autonomy for regions and local governments. These divisions gave rise to two political parties: the Conservatives, who aligned with centralist principles, and the Liberals, who championed federalism and progressive reforms. The rivalry between these parties would shape Colombian politics for decades, often erupting into violent conflicts.

One of the most significant social changes in the aftermath of independence was the abolition of slavery. Although the independence movement had drawn support from enslaved Africans and their descendants, the promise of liberation was slow to materialize. It was not until 1851 that slavery was officially abolished in Colombia, following years of advocacy and resistance by Afro-Colombian communities. The end of slavery marked a critical step toward equality, but systemic racism and economic disparities continued to marginalize Afro-Colombians, indigenous peoples, and other vulnerable groups. The legacy of these inequalities remains a pressing issue in Colombia today.

The economic landscape of post-independence Colombia was shaped by the transition from colonial extractive industries to agriculture and trade. Coffee emerged as the country's most important export crop, driving economic growth and shaping the social fabric of rural Colombia. The rise of the coffee industry created opportunities for landowners and entrepreneurs but also deepened class divisions, as small farmers and laborers struggled to compete in a system dominated by large estates. The expansion of the coffee economy also spurred the development of infrastructure, such as railways and ports, which facilitated trade and connected Colombia to global markets.

The cultural impact of independence was profound, as Colombians sought to forge a national identity distinct from their colonial past. Writers, artists, and intellectuals played a key role in this endeavor, drawing inspiration from the country's diverse landscapes, histories, and traditions. Figures like Jorge Isaacs, whose novel *María* captured the beauty of the Valle del Cauca, and the painter Epifanio Garay, known for his portraits of prominent Colombians, helped shape a sense of pride and belonging. The celebration of independence anniversaries, such as July 20, became important occasions for reaffirming national unity and honoring the sacrifices of those who fought for freedom.

The legacy of Colombia's independence movement is both inspiring and complex. It represents a triumph of resilience and determination in the face of colonial oppression, as well as the challenges of building a just and inclusive society. The ideals of liberty and self-determination that inspired the revolution continue to resonate, reminding Colombians of the importance of striving for equality, justice, and unity. The story of independence is not just a chapter in the past—it is a living narrative that shapes the country's present and future. For those who walk the streets of Bogotá, visit the historic battlefields of Boyacá, or explore the cultural heritage of Cartagena, the echoes of this transformative era are ever-present, a reminder of the enduring spirit of the Colombian people.

# The Impact of Coffee: Colombia's Role in the Coffee Trade

Colombia's relationship with coffee is as deep and rich as the brew itself. Known worldwide for producing some of the finest and most aromatic coffee beans, Colombia's role in the global coffee trade has shaped its economy, culture, and identity in profound ways. From the verdant slopes of the Andes to bustling port cities, the coffee industry has been a cornerstone of the nation's development for over a century. Its impact is woven into the fabric of Colombia's history, influencing the livelihoods of millions, the structure of society, and the country's global reputation. To understand Colombia's coffee trade is to understand a key part of what makes the nation unique.

The origins of coffee cultivation in Colombia trace back to the early 18th century, when Jesuit priests introduced the crop to the region. Initially grown on small plots for local consumption, coffee slowly gained a foothold as a viable agricultural product in rural communities. The plant's adaptability to Colombia's varied landscapes and climates made it an ideal crop for widespread cultivation. By the 19th century, coffee production had expanded significantly, driven by growing international demand and the recognition of Colombia's ideal conditions for producing high-quality Arabica beans.

Colombia's geography plays a crucial role in its coffee excellence. The Andes mountains, which run through the heart of the country, break into three distinct ranges that create a diverse array of microclimates. Factors such as altitude, temperature, humidity, and soil composition vary across these regions, allowing for the cultivation of coffee beans with unique flavor profiles. Most Colombian coffee is grown between 1,200 and 2,200 meters above sea level, where cool nights and warm days provide the perfect environment for the slow maturation of coffee cherries. This slow growth allows the beans to develop their characteristic acidity and complex flavors, qualities that distinguish Colombian coffee on the global stage.

The country's coffee-growing regions, collectively known as the Coffee Triangle or Eje Cafetero, include the departments of Caldas, Quindío, and Risaralda, though coffee is also grown in other areas like Antioquia, Huila, and Tolima. Each region contributes its own distinct characteristics to the nation's coffee repertoire. For example, beans from Huila are known for their bright acidity and fruity notes, while those from Antioquia often exhibit a smoother, nuttier profile. The diversity of flavors and aromas found in Colombian coffee has made it a favorite among connoisseurs and a staple in specialty coffee markets around the world.

The rise of coffee as an export commodity in Colombia coincided with the country's efforts to modernize its economy in the late 19th and early 20th centuries. Coffee quickly became Colombia's most important export, surpassing other commodities like tobacco and gold. The industry's growth was fueled by strong global demand, particularly from the United States and Europe, where Colombian coffee gained a reputation for its superior quality. By the mid-20th century, coffee accounted for a significant portion of Colombia's GDP and export earnings, earning it the nickname "the coffee republic."

The success of Colombia's coffee trade can also be attributed to the efforts of the Federación Nacional de Cafeteros de Colombia (FNC), or National Federation of Coffee Growers, established in 1927. The FNC was created to protect the interests of coffee farmers and promote Colombian coffee internationally. It has played a pivotal role in maintaining quality standards, supporting rural development, and building the global brand of Colombian coffee. One of the FNC's most iconic achievements is the creation of Juan Valdez, a fictional coffee farmer who became the face of Colombian coffee in marketing campaigns. Dressed in traditional clothing and accompanied by his mule, Conchita, Juan Valdez symbolizes the dedication and authenticity of Colombia's coffee producers, helping to cement the country's reputation as a leader in the industry.

While coffee has brought significant economic benefits to Colombia, its impact on society is complex and multifaceted. The industry has provided livelihoods for millions of Colombians, particularly in rural areas where other economic opportunities are limited. Smallholder farmers, who account for the majority of coffee production in Colombia, play a vital role in the industry. These farmers often work on family-owned plots of land, cultivating coffee as both a source of income and a way of life. However, the reliance on small-scale production also poses challenges, as farmers are vulnerable to fluctuations in global coffee prices, climate change, and other external factors.

The volatility of the coffee market has been a persistent issue for Colombian producers. Global coffee prices are influenced by a range of factors, including supply and demand dynamics, currency fluctuations, and speculative trading. For smallholder farmers, these price swings can mean the difference between financial stability and hardship. In response, initiatives such as fair trade certification and direct trade relationships have emerged to provide more stable and equitable income for coffee growers. These programs often involve paying premiums for high-quality beans and investing in community development projects, helping to create a more sustainable future for coffee-producing regions.

Climate change poses another significant threat to Colombia's coffee industry. Rising temperatures, unpredictable rainfall patterns, and the spread of pests and diseases, such as coffee leaf rust, have made it increasingly difficult for farmers to maintain consistent yields and quality. Some coffee-growing regions that were once ideal for cultivation are becoming less suitable due to these environmental changes. To address these challenges, Colombian coffee farmers and organizations are adopting innovative practices, such as planting disease-resistant coffee varieties, implementing agroforestry systems, and improving water management techniques. Research institutions like Cenicafé, the FNC's scientific arm, are at the forefront of these efforts, working to ensure the long-term sustainability of Colombia's coffee sector.

Beyond its economic and environmental impact, coffee is deeply ingrained in Colombia's cultural identity. The daily ritual of brewing and sharing a cup of coffee, known locally as tinto, is a cherished tradition that transcends social and economic boundaries. Coffee is more than a beverage in

Colombia—it is a symbol of hospitality, a source of pride, and a connection to the land. Festivals celebrating coffee, such as the National Coffee Festival in Quindío and the Coffee Cultural Landscape, a UNESCO World Heritage Site, highlight the significance of coffee in Colombian culture and heritage.

The Coffee Cultural Landscape, recognized by UNESCO in 2011, encompasses the picturesque coffee-growing regions of Caldas, Quindío, Risaralda, and Valle del Cauca. This designation celebrates not only the stunning landscapes of rolling hills and coffee plantations but also the traditional practices and way of life of the communities that cultivate coffee. The region's architecture, including traditional farmhouses with colorful façades and balconies, reflects the cultural heritage of the coffee industry. Visitors to the Coffee Cultural Landscape can experience the region's charm through coffee farm tours, tastings, and immersive cultural activities.

In recent years, Colombia has embraced the global specialty coffee movement, which emphasizes high-quality beans, sustainable practices, and unique flavor profiles. Specialty coffee shops and roasters have proliferated in cities like Bogotá, Medellín, and Cartagena, showcasing the diversity of Colombian coffee and introducing consumers to the stories behind the beans. This shift toward specialty coffee has opened new opportunities for farmers to command higher prices for their crops, provided they meet the exacting standards of quality and traceability demanded by the market.

Colombia's role in the coffee trade is a story of innovation, resilience, and tradition. From the small farms of the Coffee Triangle to the bustling export hubs, the country's coffee industry is a testament to the dedication and skill of its people. While challenges such as market volatility and climate change continue to pose risks, the industry's adaptability and commitment to quality have ensured that Colombian coffee remains a cherished commodity worldwide. For those who savor a cup of Colombian coffee, each sip is a connection to the land, the culture, and the generations of farmers who have made it possible. Whether enjoyed in a bustling café or on a quiet veranda overlooking the Andes, Colombian coffee is more than a drink—it is an experience, a legacy, and a symbol of a nation's enduring spirit.

## Music and Dance: Cumbia, Salsa, and Vallenato

Colombia's vibrant music and dance traditions are inseparable from its cultural identity, weaving together centuries of history, diverse influences, and regional flavors into a tapestry of sound and movement. From the soulful rhythms of cumbia to the infectious energy of salsa and the storytelling charms of vallenato, these genres embody the heart and soul of a nation. Each step, each note, and each beat carries echoes of Colombia's complex past and diverse heritage, blending African, Indigenous, and European elements into expressions that transcend language and geography. Music and dance in Colombia are not just forms of entertainment—they are lifelines to traditions, celebrations of community, and powerful symbols of resilience and joy.

Cumbia, often considered the quintessential Colombian rhythm, originated on the country's Caribbean coast, where African, Indigenous, and Spanish influences converged. Its roots stretch back to the days of colonialism, when enslaved Africans brought their drums and rhythms to the shores of Colombia. Over time, these rhythms merged with Indigenous melodies and Spanish instrumentation, giving birth to a genre that is as dynamic as the cultures that created it. Cumbia's signature sound is driven by the interplay of drums, flutes, and vocals, creating a hypnotic rhythm that invites both dancers and listeners to lose themselves in its sway.

The dance that accompanies cumbia is as captivating as the music itself. Traditionally performed in pairs, the movements are elegant and grounded, with the dancers maintaining a respectful distance while conveying a sense of courtship. Women wear flowing skirts adorned with vibrant colors and patterns, which they use to accentuate their movements, while men often dress in white with red scarves, evoking a sense of tradition and celebration. The dance reflects the blending of cultures, with Indigenous footwork, African rhythms, and Spanish influences coming together to tell a story of unity and harmony. Today, cumbia has transcended its coastal origins, becoming a symbol of Colombian identity recognized and celebrated across the country and beyond.

Salsa, on the other hand, is a genre that arrived in Colombia from abroad but has since been embraced and transformed into a distinctly Colombian expression. Originating in the Caribbean and flourishing in cities like New York and Havana, salsa found fertile ground in Colombia during the mid-20th century. The port city of Buenaventura and the bustling metropolis of Cali became hubs for this infectious genre, with their vibrant Afro-Colombian communities infusing salsa with their own unique flavor. While salsa's roots are deeply tied to the African diaspora, its adoption in Colombia reflects the country's openness to new influences and its ability to make them its own.

Cali, often referred to as the "Salsa Capital of the World," is the beating heart of salsa in Colombia. The city's love affair with salsa is evident in its dance schools, nightclubs, and annual festivals, such as the Feria de Cali, which draws dancers and musicians from around the globe. Salsa in Cali is characterized by its speed, precision, and energy, with dancers executing intricate footwork and spins at breathtaking tempos. The city's salsa style is as much about athleticism as it is about artistry, with competitions showcasing the incredible skill and creativity of its performers. For many Caleños, salsa is more than a pastime—it is a way of life, a language of expression, and a source of pride.

Vallenato, a genre born in the valleys of Colombia's northern coast, stands apart for its storytelling tradition and deep emotional resonance. Rooted in the rural landscapes of Cesar and La Guajira departments, vallenato emerged as a way for traveling minstrels, known as juglares, to share news, tales, and emotions through song. These juglares carried their accordions, guitars, and guacharacas (a percussion instrument made from a dried gourd) from village to village, weaving narratives that captured the joys, sorrows, and struggles of everyday life. Vallenato's lyrics are often poetic and deeply personal, reflecting the experiences and values of the communities it represents.

The accordion, introduced to Colombia by German immigrants in the 19th century, is the defining instrument of vallenato, lending the genre its distinctive sound. Its melodies, combined with the rhythmic strumming of the caja vallenata (a small drum) and the scraping of the guacharaca, create a musical texture that is both lively and evocative. Vallenato is divided into four traditional rhythms or airs: paseo, merengue, puya, and son, each with its own tempo and mood. These rhythms provide the foundation for vallenato's storytelling, allowing singers to convey a wide range of emotions, from exuberant celebration to heartfelt lament.

One of the most enduring figures in the history of vallenato is Carlos Vives, a Colombian singer and actor who brought the genre to international prominence in the 1990s. Vives's innovative fusion of traditional vallenato with elements of rock, pop, and other modern styles introduced a new generation to the genre while honoring its roots. His album *Clásicos de la Provincia* became a cultural phenomenon, revitalizing vallenato and cementing its place on the global stage. Vives's success is a testament to the enduring appeal of vallenato and its ability to evolve while remaining true to its essence.

The cultural significance of music and dance in Colombia extends beyond the individual genres of cumbia, salsa, and vallenato. These art forms are deeply intertwined with the country's social fabric, serving as vehicles for community building, resistance, and celebration. In times of hardship, music and dance have provided Colombians with a means of expressing their resilience and hope. Festivals, parades, and carnivals across the country showcase the diversity and creativity of its musical traditions, from the Carnaval de Barranquilla, with its cumbia performances, to the Festival de la Leyenda Vallenata, which honors the rich heritage of vallenato.

The influence of Colombian music and dance has also reached far beyond its borders, contributing to the global appreciation of Latin American culture. Artists like Shakira, who infuses her pop music with Colombian rhythms, and J Balvin, a reggaeton superstar with roots in Medellín, have introduced international audiences to the vibrancy of Colombia's musical landscape. These contemporary artists draw inspiration from their cultural heritage, demonstrating the enduring power of music and dance to connect people across time and space.

Colombia's musical traditions continue to evolve, reflecting the dynamic and diverse nature of its society. Younger generations are blending traditional genres with modern influences, creating new sounds that honor the past while embracing the future. This fusion is evident in genres like champeta, which combines African rhythms with Caribbean and urban elements, and in collaborations between traditional musicians and electronic producers. These innovations ensure that Colombia's music and dance remain relevant and vibrant, a living testament to the creativity and spirit of its people.

The rhythms and movements of cumbia, salsa, and vallenato are more than just forms of entertainment—they are expressions of identity, history, and humanity. Each genre tells a story of adaptation, resilience, and celebration, capturing the essence of Colombia's diverse culture. Whether performed on a crowded dance floor, at a community festival, or in the quiet intimacy of a family gathering, these traditions remind us of the power of music and dance to unite, inspire, and transcend. For anyone who has felt the pull of a cumbia beat, the exhilaration of salsa, or the emotion of a vallenato ballad, the magic of Colombia's music and dance is undeniable. It is a gift to the world and a source of pride for the nation that gave it life.

## Celebrations and Festivals: Carnival, Feria de las Flores, and More

Colombia's celebrations and festivals are a vivid expression of its cultural diversity, historical richness, and unrelenting joy for life. Across its regions, each festival tells a story, blending indigenous traditions, African influences, European customs, and modern creativity into unique and unforgettable experiences. These events are not only moments of collective celebration but also essential windows into the soul of the Colombian people. From the colorful chaos of Carnival to the breathtaking beauty of the Feria de las Flores and countless other regional festivities, Colombia's calendar is a testament to its exuberance, resilience, and cultural pride.

The Carnival of Barranquilla, one of the most iconic festivals in Colombia and the second-largest carnival in the world after Rio de Janeiro's, is a dazzling explosion of color, music, and traditions. Held during the four days leading up to Ash Wednesday, this UNESCO-recognized event transforms the city of Barranquilla into a living stage. The streets come alive with parades, costumes, and performances that showcase the country's rich cultural heritage. Originating from a mixture of European pre-Lenten festivities, African rhythms, and indigenous customs, the Carnival represents the vibrant fusion that defines Colombia.

The heart of the Carnival is its parades, the most famous being the Batalla de Flores (Battle of Flowers), which marks the official opening of the festivities. This parade is a visual spectacle of floats adorned with intricate designs, vibrant costumes, and performers dancing to the contagious beats of cumbia, mapalé, and other traditional rhythms. The Marimondas, mischievous characters dressed in colorful jumpsuits and grotesque masks, are a highlight of the event, embodying the playful and rebellious spirit of the Carnival. Another key moment is the Gran Parada de Tradición, which emphasizes the preservation of traditional dances and costumes, offering a glimpse into the cultural roots of the region.

For the people of Barranquilla, the Carnival is more than a celebration—it is a way of life. Preparations begin months in advance, with the entire city coming together to plan, rehearse, and create. The festival is a source of immense pride, uniting communities and generations in a shared experience of joy and creativity. Visitors from around the world are welcomed with open arms, invited to join the revelry and immerse themselves in the rhythms, flavors, and warmth of the Caribbean coast.

In stark contrast to the raucous energy of the Carnival, the Feria de las Flores (Festival of Flowers) in Medellín is a celebration of beauty, tradition, and the enduring spirit of the Antioquia region. Held annually in early August, this week-long event is a tribute to the region's flower growers, or silleteros, who have cultivated one of Colombia's most important industries. The highlight of the Feria is the Desfile de Silleteros (Silleteros Parade), where flower growers carry elaborate floral arrangements on wooden frames, or silletas, strapped to their backs. Each arrangement is a masterpiece, meticulously crafted to showcase vibrant colors, intricate designs, and messages of love, unity, or humor.

The origins of the Feria de las Flores date back to 1957, when it was introduced as a way to honor the region's flower-growing heritage and promote Medellín as a center of culture and innovation. Over the years, the festival has grown to include a diverse array of events, from concerts and art exhibitions to horse parades and gastronomic fairs. The city is transformed into a floral wonderland, with blooms adorning public spaces, homes, and businesses. Beyond its aesthetic appeal, the Feria de las Flores is a celebration of resilience, reflecting the pride and determination of the Antioqueños who have turned Medellín into a symbol of transformation and hope.

While the Carnival of Barranquilla and Feria de las Flores are among the most famous festivals in Colombia, they are just two examples of the country's rich tapestry of celebrations. Each region has its own traditions, shaped by its history, geography, and cultural influences. In the southwestern city of Pasto, the Carnaval de Negros y Blancos (Carnival of Blacks and Whites) is a unique event that celebrates diversity and unity. Held in early January, this festival has its roots in indigenous rituals and colonial-era celebrations. Participants paint their faces black one day and white the next, symbolizing racial harmony and the blending of cultures. The parade of floats, known for its elaborate and surreal designs, is a highlight of the event, showcasing the creativity and humor of the people of Pasto.

In the coffee-growing region of Armenia, the Fiesta Nacional del Café (National Coffee Festival) pays homage to the crop that has shaped Colombia's history and identity. This festival, held in late June or early July, features coffee-themed parades, beauty pageants, and traditional music performances. The event is a celebration of the hard work and dedication of the coffee farmers, who play a vital role in the country's economy and culture. Visitors can immerse themselves in the sights, sounds, and flavors of the Coffee Triangle, gaining a deeper appreciation for the region's heritage and way of life.

On the Caribbean island of San Andrés, the Green Moon Festival is a vibrant celebration of Afro-Caribbean culture, music, and food. This festival, held in September, highlights the island's unique identity, shaped by its history as a crossroads of African, European, and Indigenous influences. The event features reggae and calypso concerts, traditional dance performances, and culinary showcases that reflect the island's rich cultural heritage. The Green Moon Festival is a testament to the resilience and creativity of the Raizal community, who have preserved their traditions and language despite centuries of external pressures.

In the Andes, the Festival Internacional de Música de Cartagena brings a different kind of celebration to the historic port city. Held in January, this classical music festival attracts world-renowned musicians and ensembles, offering a sophisticated and intimate experience for music lovers. The performances take place in stunning venues, such as the Teatro Adolfo Mejía and the colonial churches of Cartagena's walled city, creating an atmosphere of elegance and reverence. The festival is a reminder of Colombia's diverse cultural offerings, showcasing its ability to embrace both tradition and innovation.

Colombian festivals are not only a feast for the senses but also a reflection of the country's resilience and strength. Many festivals have emerged as acts of defiance against adversity, using music, dance, and art to heal wounds and build bridges. The Festival de la Leyenda Vallenata in Valledupar, for example, celebrates the storytelling tradition of vallenato music, a genre that has long been a voice for the people of the Magdalena River Valley. Similarly, the Carnaval de Riosucio in Caldas is rooted in indigenous resistance to Spanish colonization, blending satire and spirituality into a unique and powerful expression of identity.

The impact of these festivals extends far beyond their immediate participants, contributing to Colombia's economy, tourism, and international reputation. Each year, millions of visitors flock to the country to experience its celebrations, bringing economic benefits to local communities and fostering cross-cultural exchange. The festivals also serve as platforms for preserving and promoting Colombia's traditions, ensuring that its diverse heritage remains vibrant and relevant in a rapidly changing world.

The magic of Colombian festivals lies in their ability to unite people across differences, creating moments of shared joy and connection. Whether you are dancing in the streets of Barranquilla, marveling at the floral creations in Medellín, or savoring the rhythms of vallenato in Valledupar, you are participating in a celebration that transcends boundaries and reminds us of the beauty of human creativity and resilience. These festivals are not only a testament to Colombia's cultural richness but also a source of inspiration for anyone who believes in the power of art, community, and tradition to bring people together.

# Indigenous Cultures: Preserving Traditions in a Modern World

Colombia's indigenous cultures are a vital thread in the intricate tapestry of the nation's identity, representing thousands of years of history, resilience, and adaptation. Long before the Spanish conquest, Colombia was home to a multitude of indigenous peoples, each with their own languages, traditions, and ways of life. Today, despite centuries of colonization, conflict, and modern pressures, many of these cultures continue to thrive, preserving their ancestral knowledge and practices while navigating the challenges of a rapidly changing world. The story of Colombia's indigenous communities is one of survival and resistance, but also of profound contributions to the country's cultural and environmental heritage.

The diversity of Colombia's indigenous peoples is staggering, with over 100 distinct groups recognized today, speaking more than 60 different languages. These communities are scattered across the country, from the snow-capped peaks of the Sierra Nevada de Santa Marta to the dense rainforests of the Amazon and the arid deserts of La Guajira. Each group is deeply connected to its environment, drawing sustenance, spirituality, and identity from the land. For example, the Kogi, Wiwa, Arhuaco, and Kankuamo peoples of the Sierra Nevada view themselves as guardians of the Earth, entrusted with maintaining its balance through rituals and sustainable practices. Their worldview, known as the "Law of Origin," emphasizes harmony between humanity and nature, a philosophy that holds valuable lessons for our modern era.

One of the most visible symbols of Colombia's indigenous heritage is the mamo, a spiritual leader found among the Kogi and other Sierra Nevada communities. Mamos are chosen at a young age and undergo years of rigorous training, often in seclusion, to develop their understanding of the spiritual and natural worlds. They play a central role in guiding their communities, performing rituals to restore balance and offering wisdom on matters ranging from agriculture to conflict resolution. The mamos' teachings, rooted in ancestral knowledge, serve as a reminder of the deep connection between humans and the environment—a connection that is increasingly threatened by deforestation, mining, and climate change.

In the southern region of the Amazon, indigenous groups such as the Tikuna, Huitoto, and Yucuna have maintained their traditional ways of life despite encroaching modernity. The Amazon rainforest is not only their home but also a sacred space teeming with life and spiritual significance. These communities rely on the forest for food, medicine, and shelter, using their extensive knowledge of plants and animals to sustain themselves while preserving the ecosystem. Traditional practices such as slash-and-burn agriculture are carefully managed to minimize environmental impact, reflecting a deep understanding of ecological balance. However, illegal logging, oil exploration, and land grabbing pose significant threats to the Amazon and its indigenous inhabitants, forcing them to defend their territories and advocate for their rights.

In the Guajira Peninsula, the Wayuu people have adapted to one of Colombia's harshest environments, a desert landscape where water is scarce, and temperatures soar. The Wayuu are known for their vibrant cultural expressions, including their intricate weaving traditions. Wayuu women create stunning hammocks, bags, and textiles, each piece telling a story through its patterns and colors. These crafts are not only a source of income but also a way of preserving cultural identity in the face of modernization. The Wayuu have also developed unique systems of social organization, with matrilineal clans playing a central role in community life. Despite their resilience, the Wayuu face challenges such as water scarcity, poverty, and inadequate access to healthcare and education, underscoring the need for greater support and recognition.

The preservation of indigenous languages is a crucial aspect of safeguarding Colombia's cultural heritage. Language is more than a means of communication; it is a repository of history, knowledge, and identity. Many indigenous languages in Colombia are endangered, with younger generations increasingly adopting Spanish as their primary language. Efforts to revitalize these languages are gaining momentum, with initiatives such as bilingual education programs and the documentation of oral traditions. For instance, the Nasa people of the Cauca region have established schools that teach both Spanish and their native language, Nasa Yuwe, ensuring that future generations remain connected to their roots. These efforts highlight the importance of linguistic diversity in maintaining the cultural richness of Colombia.

Indigenous art and music are powerful expressions of identity and spirituality, reflecting the values and beliefs of their creators. In the Amazon, the maloca, or communal house, serves as a symbolic and physical space for artistic and musical traditions. Rituals held in the maloca often feature intricate body painting, feathered headdresses, and rhythmic drumming, creating a multisensory experience that connects participants to their ancestors and the natural world. In the Sierra Nevada, the Kogi use sacred objects such as poporos—lime-filled gourds used in spiritual practices—as symbols of their connection to the cosmos. These artistic and ritualistic expressions are not merely decorative; they are imbued with meaning and serve as a link between the past and the present.

The relationship between indigenous communities and the Colombian state has been fraught with tension and struggle. For much of Colombia's history, indigenous peoples were marginalized, their lands taken, and their rights ignored. However, significant progress has been made in recent decades. The 1991 Colombian Constitution marked a turning point, recognizing Colombia as a multicultural and pluri-ethnic nation and granting indigenous communities greater autonomy over their territories. This legal recognition has empowered indigenous groups to assert their rights and protect their lands from external threats. Indigenous leaders have also become increasingly active in national politics, advocating for policies that address their communities' needs and priorities.

Despite these advancements, challenges remain. Land disputes, violence, and resource extraction continue to threaten indigenous territories, often putting communities at odds with powerful economic and political interests. In regions such as Cauca and Chocó, indigenous activists have faced violence and persecution for defending their rights. The global demand for natural resources, coupled with weak enforcement of environmental protections, has exacerbated these conflicts. Indigenous communities are often on the frontlines of these struggles, fighting not only for their survival but also for the preservation of Colombia's natural heritage.

Education plays a pivotal role in preserving indigenous cultures while equipping younger generations to navigate the modern world. Many indigenous communities have embraced intercultural education, which integrates traditional knowledge with formal schooling. This approach allows students to learn about their heritage while gaining the skills needed to engage with broader society. In the Amazon, for example, schools teach students how to identify medicinal plants and understand ecological systems, alongside subjects like math and science. This holistic approach fosters a sense of pride and belonging while preparing indigenous youth to become leaders and advocates for their communities.

The resilience of Colombia's indigenous peoples is a testament to their strength and determination. From the mist-shrouded peaks of the Andes to the dense jungles of the Amazon, these communities have endured centuries of upheaval while maintaining their traditions and values. Their wisdom, creativity, and connection to the land are invaluable not only to Colombia but to the world. In an era of environmental crisis and cultural homogenization, the lessons and perspectives of indigenous cultures offer a path toward sustainability, diversity, and harmony.

Preserving indigenous traditions is not just an act of cultural conservation; it is an affirmation of the dignity and humanity of Colombia's first peoples. Their voices, stories, and practices enrich the nation's identity, reminding us of the deep roots that anchor Colombia's past and the possibilities that lie ahead. By supporting indigenous communities, respecting their rights, and valuing their contributions, Colombia can ensure that these traditions continue to thrive, offering inspiration and guidance for generations to come.

# CHAPTER 4: CULINARY DELIGHTS OF COLOMBIA

## Regional Flavors: From the Caribbean Coast to the Andes

Colombian cuisine is as diverse as its landscapes and cultures, with each region offering a distinct palette of flavors, ingredients, and culinary traditions. From the sun-soaked Caribbean coast to the cool, misty highlands of the Andes, Colombia's culinary map reflects the rich interplay of indigenous, African, and Spanish influences, as well as the unique qualities of the land itself. Each region tells a story through its food—a story of adaptation, creativity, and the deep connection between people and their environment. Exploring Colombian cuisine is not just about savoring delicious dishes; it is about understanding the heart of its communities and the history that has shaped them.

On the Caribbean coast, the cuisine bursts with vibrant flavors that echo the region's Afro-Caribbean heritage and tropical abundance. Fresh seafood is a cornerstone of the coastal diet, with dishes like cazuela de mariscos (seafood stew) and pargo frito (fried red snapper) showcasing the bounty of the sea. These dishes are often accompanied by coconut rice, made by cooking rice with coconut milk and a touch of sugar, resulting in a creamy and slightly sweet side that perfectly complements the savory main courses. Another coastal favorite is patacones, green plantains that are fried, smashed, and fried again to create crispy discs that serve as a versatile base or side.

The influence of African culinary traditions is particularly evident in dishes like arroz con coco and sopa de mondongo (tripe soup), as well as in the use of bold spices and seasonings. Street vendors are a common sight along the Caribbean coast, offering treats like arepas de huevo—cornmeal patties stuffed with egg and sometimes meat or cheese—and cocadas, sweet coconut-based confections. The coastal city of Cartagena is a food lover's paradise, where colonial-era charm meets a dynamic food scene that highlights both traditional recipes and modern interpretations. In Cartagena's bustling Bazurto Market, the energy is palpable, with vendors calling out their offerings of fresh fish, tropical fruits like lulo and guanábana, and fragrant herbs like cilantro and culantro.

Moving inland to the fertile lowlands of the Magdalena River Valley, the cuisine shifts to reflect the agricultural wealth of the region. This area is known for its production of tropical fruits, including bananas, mangoes, and papayas, which feature prominently in both desserts and savory dishes. One of the most iconic dishes of this region is sancocho, a hearty stew made with a variety of meats, root vegetables like yucca and potatoes, and plantains. Sancocho is a dish that transcends regions, with each area putting its own spin on the recipe, but in the Magdalena Valley, it is often prepared with fish, reflecting the proximity to rivers and the coast.

As the land begins to rise into the Andes, the flavors of Colombia take on a heartier and earthier quality, mirroring the cool climate and rugged terrain. The Andean region, home to cities like Bogotá, Medellín, and Manizales, is known for its comfort foods and reliance on ingredients like potatoes, corn, and meat. Ajiaco, a traditional soup from the capital city of Bogotá, is a quintessential Andean dish that combines three types of potatoes with chicken, corn, and a fragrant herb called guasca. Served with avocado, capers, and a dollop of cream, ajiaco is a warming and satisfying meal that reflects the highland environment.

Empanadas are another staple of the Andean region, with variations found in nearly every corner of the country. These pastries are typically filled with a mixture of meat, potatoes, and spices, then fried to golden perfection. In Medellín, the empanadas might be smaller and spicier, while in Bogotá, they are often larger and paired with aji, a tangy and spicy sauce made from cilantro, green onion, and chili peppers. Arepas, a versatile cornmeal flatbread, are ubiquitous in the Andes and across Colombia, serving as a base for toppings or as a side to hearty meals. Each region has its own version of arepas, from the thicker, cheese-filled arepas boyacenses of Boyacá to the thinner, crispier arepas antioqueñas of Antioquia.

The coffee-growing regions of the Andes, collectively known as the Coffee Triangle, add another layer of flavor to Colombian cuisine. Beyond producing some of the world's finest coffee, this region is also known for its dishes that highlight the simplicity and freshness of locally sourced ingredients. Bandeja paisa, a generous platter that originated in Antioquia, is perhaps the most iconic dish of the Coffee Triangle. This feast includes beans, rice, ground beef, chorizo, fried egg, avocado, and chicharrón (crispy pork belly), all served on a single plate. It is a celebration of abundance and hard work, embodying the spirit of the region's farming communities.

In Colombia's eastern plains, known as Los Llanos, the cuisine reflects the traditions of cattle ranching and the vast, open landscapes. This region is famous for its asado llanero, a style of barbecue that involves skewering large cuts of beef, pork, or chicken on wooden stakes and roasting them over an open fire. The result is smoky, tender meat that is often served with yuca, plantains, and a spicy sauce called chimichurri. The Llanos region also boasts exotic ingredients like capybara and river fish, which are prepared using time-honored techniques passed down through generations.

To the south, in the Amazon rainforest, the cuisine takes on an entirely different character, drawing from the incredible biodiversity of the region. Indigenous communities have long relied on the forest for sustenance, using ingredients like cassava, plantains, and fish in their cooking. One of the most distinctive Amazonian dishes is pescado moqueado, fish wrapped in banana leaves and roasted over a fire, which infuses the fish with a smoky aroma and tender texture. Exotic fruits like camu camu and copoazú add a unique sweetness to both savory dishes and desserts, providing a taste of the Amazon's unparalleled natural richness.

Colombian cuisine is also notable for its beverages, which vary by region and reflect the country's agricultural abundance. In the Andes, you'll find aguapanela, a comforting drink made from panela (unrefined cane sugar) dissolved in hot water, often served with a wedge of lime or a piece of cheese for dipping. Along the coast, tropical fruit juices like maracuyá (passion fruit) and tamarindo (tamarind) are refreshing accompaniments to meals. And, of course, no exploration of Colombian beverages would be complete without mentioning coffee. Whether enjoyed as a simple tinto (black coffee) or as part of a sophisticated brew in a specialty café, Colombian coffee is a source of national pride and a testament to the country's agricultural excellence.

Desserts in Colombia are as diverse as its savory dishes, with each region offering its own sweet specialties. On the Caribbean coast, you'll find cocadas and enyucado, a cassava-based dessert flavored with coconut and anise. In the Andes, desserts like arequipe (similar to dulce de leche) and natilla, a custard-like treat often enjoyed during Christmas, are staples of traditional celebrations. The Coffee Triangle is known for its postre de natas, a creamy dessert made from the skin that forms on boiled milk, sweetened with sugar and cinnamon. These desserts, like the savory dishes that precede them, reflect Colombia's ability to turn simple ingredients into something extraordinary.

The regional flavors of Colombia are not just about food—they are about the people, histories, and landscapes that give each dish its unique character. Every bite tells a story, whether it's the legacy of African slaves who brought their culinary traditions to the coast, the ingenuity of indigenous farmers who cultivated the land for centuries, or the Spanish influences that introduced new ingredients and techniques. Colombian cuisine is a celebration of diversity and creativity, a reflection of the country's resilience and its ability to find joy and beauty in every corner of life. To explore Colombia through its food is to embark on a journey of discovery, one that leaves an indelible mark on both the palate and the soul.

# Must-Try Dishes: Arepas, Bandeja Paisa, and Ajiaco

Colombian cuisine is a vibrant reflection of its diverse landscapes, cultures, and histories, and among its many culinary treasures, a few dishes stand out as quintessential representations of the nation's gastronomic identity. Arepas, bandeja paisa, and ajiaco are not just meals; they are deeply rooted in the cultural fabric of the country, carrying stories of the regions and communities that created them. Each dish is an invitation to explore Colombia's rich culinary heritage and a testament to the creativity and resourcefulness of its people. To experience these dishes is to understand a piece of Colombia's soul, where food is both sustenance and celebration.

Arepas are perhaps the most iconic and versatile food in Colombia, a staple that transcends regional boundaries and appears on tables across the country. Made from cornmeal, water, and salt, arepas are deceptively simple yet endlessly adaptable. Their history dates back to pre-Columbian times, when indigenous communities across the Andes cultivated maize as a central element of their diet. Over the centuries, the preparation of arepas evolved, incorporating influences from Spanish colonists and Afro-Caribbean communities, while still retaining its indigenous roots. Today, arepas are as diverse as the regions of Colombia, each with its own variation reflecting local ingredients and tastes.

In Antioquia and the Coffee Triangle, arepas are thin, white, and slightly crisp, often served as an accompaniment to meals or used to scoop up beans and meat. These arepas antioqueñas are typically made without any filling, showcasing the pure, slightly nutty flavor of the corn. In contrast, the arepas of Boyacá, known as arepas boyacenses, are thicker and richer, often stuffed with cheese and baked until golden and fluffy. On the Caribbean coast, you'll find arepas de huevo, a unique version that is deep-fried and filled with an egg, creating a satisfying combination of crispy exterior and gooey interior. The versatility of arepas makes them a canvas for creativity, whether enjoyed plain with a pat of butter, topped with avocado and shredded meat, or transformed into a hearty meal with endless possibilities.

The preparation of arepas is as much a ritual as it is a culinary process. In many homes, the day begins with the sound of corn being ground into masa, the dough that forms the base of the dish. Shaping the dough into perfect discs requires skill and patience, and cooking them on a hot griddle, or budare, demands careful attention to achieve the right balance of softness and crispness. For many Colombians, the aroma of freshly made arepas evokes memories of family gatherings, early morning breakfasts, and the comforting rhythm of daily life. It is a dish that connects generations, passed down from grandmothers to grandchildren, ensuring that the tradition endures.

Bandeja paisa, on the other hand, is a dish that embodies abundance and the spirit of the Antioquia region. This hearty platter is a celebration of the region's agricultural wealth and the hardworking culture of its people. Originating in the mountainous heartland of Colombia, bandeja paisa was traditionally a meal for farmers and laborers, designed to provide the energy needed for a long day of physical work. Over time, it has become a symbol of Colombian culinary pride, often served at special occasions and featured prominently on restaurant menus.

The components of bandeja paisa are as varied as they are indulgent. At its core, the dish includes red beans cooked with pork, white rice, ground beef, chicharrón (crispy fried pork belly), a fried egg, and slices of ripe plantain. It is typically garnished with avocado, arepas, and hogao, a tomato and onion sauce that adds a burst of flavor. Some versions also include morcilla (blood sausage) or chorizo, further enhancing the dish's richness. The beauty of bandeja paisa lies in its balance of flavors and textures: the creaminess of the beans contrasts with the crunch of the chicharrón, while the sweetness of the plantains complements the savory elements.

Eating bandeja paisa is an experience that goes beyond taste. The sheer size of the plate, often served on a large wooden tray, is both a challenge and a delight. Sharing this meal with friends or family is a common practice, fostering a sense of community and camaraderie. For visitors to Colombia, trying bandeja paisa is almost a rite of passage, an opportunity to immerse oneself in the traditions and flavors of the Antioquia region. It is a dish that reflects the warmth and generosity of Colombian hospitality, leaving a lasting impression on anyone who tries it.

Ajiaco, a traditional soup from Bogotá and the Andean highlands, offers a different perspective on Colombian cuisine, one that is deeply tied to the climate and culture of the region. This comforting dish is a testament to the ingenuity of highland communities, who made use of the ingredients available to them to create a meal that is both nourishing and flavorful. At its heart, ajiaco is a potato soup, but it is far more than the sum of its parts.

The defining feature of ajiaco is the use of three types of potatoes: criolla, sabanera, and pastusa. Each variety contributes a unique texture and flavor to the soup, with the criolla potatoes breaking down to create a creamy base, while the sabanera and pastusa potatoes add heartiness. The soup also includes chicken, corn on the cob, and guasca, a native herb that imparts a distinct earthy aroma. Ajiaco is traditionally served with a variety of accompaniments, including capers, heavy cream, avocado, and rice, allowing each diner to customize their bowl to their liking.

The preparation of ajiaco is a labor of love, requiring hours of simmering to achieve the perfect balance of flavors. It is a dish that is often associated with family gatherings and celebrations, bringing people together around a steaming pot of soup. In Bogotá, ajiaco is a staple of both home cooking and restaurant menus, cherished for its ability to warm the body and soul on a chilly highland day. For Colombians, it is more than just a meal—it is a taste of home, a reminder of the Andean roots that run deep in the nation's history.

The cultural significance of these dishes extends beyond their ingredients and preparation. They are symbols of Colombia's regional diversity, each one telling a story of the land and the people who shaped it. Arepas, bandeja paisa, and ajiaco are not just foods; they are expressions of identity, heritage, and community. They remind us of the importance of preserving culinary traditions in the face of globalization and modernity, ensuring that future generations can continue to enjoy the flavors and stories that define Colombia.

To experience these dishes is to take a journey through Colombia's landscapes and histories, from the bustling streets of Bogotá to the verdant hills of Antioquia and the sun-drenched Caribbean coast. Each bite is an opportunity to connect with the people and places that make Colombia so unique. Whether you're savoring the simplicity of an arepa, marveling at the abundance of a bandeja paisa, or finding comfort in the warmth of ajiaco, these dishes offer a window into the heart of Colombian culture. They are a celebration of flavor, tradition, and the enduring power of food to bring people together.

## Coffee Culture: From Bean to Cup in the Coffee Triangle

Colombia's Coffee Triangle, or Eje Cafetero, is an enchanting region that lies at the heart of the nation's identity and reputation as one of the world's premier coffee producers. Located in the departments of Caldas, Quindío, and Risaralda, this lush area is defined by its verdant hills, meticulously cultivated coffee plantations, and a culture that revolves around the bean. Coffee is more than just an agricultural product in this region—it is a way of life, a tradition passed down through generations, and a source of pride for the communities who dedicate their lives to its cultivation. From the moment a coffee cherry is plucked from the branch to the final pour into a cup, Colombian coffee tells a story of craftsmanship, passion, and connection to the land.

The journey of coffee in the Coffee Triangle begins with the soil. The rugged terrain of the Andes, combined with volcanic soils rich in nutrients, provides an ideal environment for growing high-quality Arabica beans. The region's altitude, ranging between 1,200 and 2,200 meters above sea level, ensures the cool temperatures and consistent rainfall necessary for coffee plants to thrive. This unique combination of factors allows the beans to mature slowly, developing the complex flavors and bright acidity that Colombian coffee is renowned for. Coffee farms, known locally as fincas, are often small, family-run operations that have been passed down for generations, each one carrying its own history and traditions.

The process of cultivating coffee begins with the planting of seedlings, which are carefully nurtured in shaded nurseries before being transplanted to the fields. Coffee plants typically take three to four years to mature and bear fruit, producing bright red cherries that are harvested by hand. This manual harvest is a labor-intensive process, but it ensures that only the ripest cherries are picked, preserving the quality of the final product. The skill and dedication of the coffee pickers, or recolectores, are integral to the industry, as their expertise determines the foundation of the coffee's flavor profile.

Once harvested, the cherries must be processed to extract the coffee beans. The most common method in the Coffee Triangle is the washed, or wet, process, which involves removing the pulp from the cherries and fermenting the beans to remove the sticky mucilage layer. After fermentation, the beans are thoroughly washed and then dried, either in the sun on large patios or using mechanical dryers during the rainy season. This method enhances the beans' clarity and brightness, contributing to the clean and balanced flavor that Colombian coffee is famous for. The dried beans, known as parchment coffee, are then hulled to remove their outer layer, leaving the green coffee beans that are ready for export or roasting.

Roasting is where the magic of coffee truly begins to reveal itself. In the Coffee Triangle, artisanal roasters take great care to preserve the unique characteristics of each batch of beans. The roasting process involves applying precise heat to transform the green beans into the aromatic, flavorful coffee that we recognize. Light roasts tend to highlight the beans' natural acidity and fruity notes, while darker roasts bring out richer, caramelized flavors. The skill of the roaster lies in striking the perfect balance, unlocking the beans' potential while respecting their origins.

The connection between the coffee and its origins is a central tenet of the Coffee Triangle's culture. Many farms and cooperatives participate in traceability initiatives, ensuring that each bag of coffee can be linked back to the finca where it was grown. This transparency not only supports fair trade practices but also allows consumers to appreciate the unique qualities of each region and farm. Some farms even produce micro-lots, small batches of coffee that showcase exceptional qualities and terroir-specific flavors. These micro-lots are highly sought after by specialty coffee enthusiasts, further elevating Colombia's reputation in the global coffee market.

Visiting the Coffee Triangle offers a chance to immerse oneself in the world of coffee, from its cultivation to its cultural significance. Coffee farm tours are a popular activity, allowing visitors to walk among the rows of coffee plants, observe the harvesting process, and learn about the painstaking effort that goes into each cup. Many fincas also offer hands-on experiences, such as picking cherries or participating in a cupping session, where guests can taste and evaluate different coffee profiles. These experiences provide a deeper appreciation for the work of Colombian coffee farmers and the artistry behind their craft.

The towns of the Coffee Triangle are as charming as the landscapes that surround them, each one offering its own unique connection to coffee culture. Salento, with its colorful colonial architecture and vibrant atmosphere, is a gateway to the Cocora Valley and its iconic wax palms. The town's cafés and coffee shops serve some of the best brews in the region, often accompanied by stories of local farmers and their families. Manizales, perched on the slopes of the Andes, is a bustling city that combines urban energy with a strong coffee tradition. Its annual Coffee Cultural Festival celebrates the region's heritage through music, dance, and, of course, plenty of coffee.

One of the most remarkable aspects of coffee culture in the Coffee Triangle is the sense of community that it fosters. Coffee is not just an economic activity—it is a way of life that brings people together. Farmers, pickers, roasters, and baristas all play a role in the journey from bean to cup, each contributing their expertise and passion. This interconnectedness is evident in the region's cooperatives, which provide small-scale farmers with access to resources, markets, and support networks. By working together, these communities ensure the sustainability and success of their industry while preserving their traditions for future generations.

Sustainability is a key focus for the Coffee Triangle, as the region grapples with the challenges of climate change and market volatility. Rising temperatures and unpredictable weather patterns threaten the delicate balance required for coffee cultivation, prompting farmers to adopt innovative practices to protect their crops. Shade-grown coffee, agroforestry systems, and organic farming methods are among the strategies being used to mitigate environmental impact and promote biodiversity. Organizations like the Federación Nacional de Cafeteros (National Federation of Coffee Growers) and Cenicafé, its research arm, play a crucial role in supporting these efforts, providing farmers with the knowledge and tools they need to adapt to changing conditions.

The social impact of coffee extends beyond the farms and into the broader community. The coffee industry has long been a source of economic stability and opportunity for the Coffee Triangle, providing livelihoods for thousands of families. Programs that promote education, healthcare, and infrastructure development are often funded by coffee cooperatives and organizations, ensuring that the benefits of the industry are shared widely. For many families, coffee represents not only a means of survival but also a source of pride and identity, a legacy to be passed down through generations.

In every corner of the Coffee Triangle, the aroma of freshly brewed coffee is a constant reminder of the region's heritage and its role in the world. Whether sipping a simple tinto at a roadside café or savoring a meticulously prepared pour-over in a specialty shop, each cup tells a story of dedication, resilience, and love for the land. Colombian coffee is more than just a beverage—it is a symbol of the country's spirit, a connection to its history, and a bridge between cultures. For those who have experienced the Coffee Triangle, the journey from bean to cup is not just a process—it is a celebration of life itself.

## Street Food Adventures: Empanadas, Buñuelos, and More

Colombia's bustling streets are alive with the aroma of sizzling oil, the chatter of vendors, and the irresistible allure of street food served fresh and hot from market stalls, carts, and corner shops. Street food in Colombia is not just a quick bite on the go—it's a culinary adventure that captures the heart of the country's diverse food culture. Each region, town, and city offers its own specialties, but no matter where you go, one constant remains: the passion and pride of the vendors who craft these iconic snacks. Among the most beloved offerings are empanadas and buñuelos, though these are only the beginning of a tantalizing journey through Colombia's streets.

Empanadas are an undeniable favorite, a staple of Colombian street food that transcends regional boundaries while adapting to local tastes. These golden, crescent-shaped pastries are made by stuffing seasoned fillings—most commonly beef, chicken, or cheese—into a dough made from cornmeal or wheat flour. The empanadas are then deep-fried until crisp, creating a flaky exterior that gives way to a warm, flavorful center. What sets Colombian empanadas apart is their versatility. In some areas, they're served with a spicy ají sauce, made with cilantro, green onion, and chili, which provides a tangy, refreshing kick. In others, they might include unique fillings like rice, potatoes, or even a mix of the two, creating a dish that's both satisfying and portable.

The preparation of empanadas is an art form, honed over generations and passed down through families. Vendors rise before dawn to prepare the dough, often grinding corn by hand to achieve the perfect texture. The fillings are carefully seasoned with a blend of spices, ensuring a balance of flavors that will appeal to even the most discerning palates. Watching the process is as much a part of the experience as eating the empanadas themselves. The rhythmic folding and sealing of the dough, the bubbling oil that crisps the edges, and the vendor's practiced movements all contribute to the charm of this beloved snack.

Buñuelos, on the other hand, are a completely different yet equally captivating treat. These round, golden fritters are made from a dough of yucca starch and white cheese, resulting in a texture that's light and airy on the inside but crisp on the outside. Buñuelos are especially popular during the Christmas season, but they're available year-round at street stalls and bakeries. Their slightly salty flavor, combined with the subtle sweetness of the fried dough, makes them an irresistible snack that pairs perfectly with a cup of hot chocolate or coffee. In the early mornings, it's not uncommon to see Colombians starting their day with a freshly fried buñuelo and a warm beverage in hand.

The secret to a perfect buñuelo lies in the dough. The cheese must be finely grated and evenly distributed to ensure each bite is consistent in flavor, while the yucca starch provides the elasticity needed for the dough to puff up as it fries. Vendors often fry them in large batches, using deep, wide pots filled with oil. As the buñuelos cook, they rise to the surface and spin gently, creating an even golden hue. The sight and smell of freshly fried buñuelos is enough to draw a crowd, and it's not uncommon to see people patiently waiting in line for their turn to enjoy this iconic Colombian snack.

Beyond empanadas and buñuelos, the variety of street food in Colombia is astounding, each dish offering a unique glimpse into the country's culinary heritage. Arepas, for instance, are a street food staple that comes in countless variations. From the thick, cheese-filled arepa de choclo to the thin, crispy arepa de huevo stuffed with egg and meat, each version captures a different facet of Colombian cuisine. Arepas are as much a cultural symbol as they are a food item, reflecting the ingenuity and resourcefulness of the communities that created them.

On the Caribbean coast, street food takes on a tropical flair, with dishes like carimañolas and deditos de queso stealing the spotlight. Carimañolas are similar to empanadas but made with a dough of mashed yucca, which gives them a slightly chewy texture. These are typically filled with seasoned ground beef or chicken and fried to perfection. Deditos de queso, or cheese sticks, are made by wrapping pastry dough around chunks of salty, melty cheese before frying them. Both snacks are perfect examples of how Colombian street food combines simple ingredients to create something deeply satisfying.

In cities like Bogotá and Medellín, you'll find skewers of grilled meats known as pinchos, which are a favorite among evening crowds. These skewers often feature chunks of chicken, beef, or pork, marinated in a mix of herbs and spices, then grilled over an open flame. Some vendors also include vegetables like bell peppers and onions, adding a burst of freshness to the smoky, savory meat. Pinchos are usually served with a side of arepas or small packets of chimichurri sauce, making them a hearty and flavorful option for those on the go.

For those with a sweet tooth, Colombian street food offers an array of desserts and treats that are impossible to resist. Churros, long tubes of fried dough dusted with sugar, are a classic choice, often served with a side of arequipe for dipping. Arequipe, similar to dulce de leche, is a caramel-like spread made from sweetened condensed milk that adds a rich, indulgent layer to any dessert. Another popular option is obleas, thin wafers sandwiched around arequipe, grated cheese, or fruit preserves. These delicate, crispy treats are a fun and customizable snack that's perfect for sharing.

One of the most intriguing aspects of Colombian street food is its connection to local traditions and histories. Many of these dishes have their roots in indigenous, African, and Spanish culinary practices, evolving over centuries to become what they are today. Empanadas, for example, are thought to have originated from the Spanish empanadas brought to Colombia during colonization, but they have since been adapted to suit local tastes and ingredients. Similarly, buñuelos trace their origins to Spain, yet the use of yucca starch and Colombian cheese gives them a distinctly local flavor.

The street food experience in Colombia is also deeply social. Vendors often set up shop in busy plazas, markets, or along main streets, creating spaces where people gather to eat, talk, and connect. It's not uncommon for vendors to develop loyal followings, with customers returning time and again for their favorite empanadas, buñuelos, or other specialties. The sense of community that surrounds street food is palpable, turning a simple meal into an opportunity for shared moments and cultural exchange.

What makes Colombian street food truly special is the way it reflects the character of its people—resourceful, vibrant, and welcoming. Each dish tells a story of adaptation and creativity, using humble ingredients to create something extraordinary. Whether it's the crispy edges of a perfectly fried empanada, the pillowy softness of a fresh buñuelo, or the sweet satisfaction of a churro dipped in arequipe, every bite is a testament to the skill and passion of the vendors who keep these traditions alive.

Exploring Colombian street food is more than just a culinary adventure; it's a journey into the heart of the country's culture. It's about savoring the flavors that define a region, connecting with the people who make it all possible, and discovering the stories that have shaped each dish. From the early morning aroma of fried dough to the late-night sizzle of skewers on a grill, street food captures the energy, diversity, and warmth of

Colombia in ways that no other experience can. For anyone lucky enough to walk these streets and taste these flavors, the memories will linger long after the last bite.

## Drinks to Savor: Aguardiente, Lulo Juice, and Colombian Craft Beer

Colombian beverages are as diverse and captivating as the country itself, offering a rich interplay of traditional flavors, natural ingredients, and cultural significance. From the fiery kick of aguardiente to the refreshing tang of lulo juice and the burgeoning world of Colombian craft beer, the drinks of this nation carry a story in every sip. Each one reflects the landscapes, heritage, and creativity of its people, making these beverages not just something to quench your thirst but an essential part of experiencing Colombian culture. Whether shared during a festive celebration, savored on a sunny afternoon, or paired with a hearty meal, these drinks draw you closer to the heart of Colombia.

Aguardiente is perhaps the most iconic Colombian spirit, a drink that has become synonymous with celebrations, gatherings, and a sense of camaraderie. Translating to "firewater" in English, aguardiente is a strong, anise-flavored liquor distilled from sugarcane. Its roots stretch back centuries, blending the agricultural bounty of Colombia with influences from Spain, where similar anise-flavored spirits are common. Aguardiente is a staple at parties, festivals, and family gatherings, where it is often consumed straight in small shots, accompanied by lively music and laughter. Its sharp, slightly sweet taste with a licorice-like finish may not be for everyone at first, but for Colombians, it carries the distinct flavor of joy and unity.

The production of aguardiente is a carefully regulated process, with each region of Colombia producing its own variation. Antioquia, Caldas, and Cundinamarca are particularly known for their aguardiente, and each has subtle differences in flavor and strength. Some varieties are sweeter, while others are dryer or have a stronger anise note. What unites them all is the communal experience of sharing a bottle. Aguardiente is not merely a drink—it's a social ritual, a way of breaking down barriers and bringing people together. Toasting with a round of aguardiente is a moment of connection, a symbol of friendship and celebration.

Accompanying aguardiente at many gatherings is a selection of traditional Colombian snacks, such as empanadas, chicharrones, or buñuelos. The pairing of the spirit's bold flavor with the richness of these foods creates a balance that enhances the experience. It's also common to see aguardiente enjoyed with music and dancing, especially during festive occasions like Carnival or Christmas. The drink fuels the rhythm of the night, making it as much a part of the celebration as the music and movement.

On the opposite end of the spectrum, lulo juice offers a refreshing and vibrant taste of Colombia's tropical bounty. Lulo, also known as naranjilla in other parts of Latin America, is a small, orange fruit with a tart, citrusy flavor that is often described as a mix between lime and pineapple. The fruit grows abundantly in Colombia's high-altitude regions, where the cooler climate helps to preserve its bright acidity and unique flavor profile. Lulo juice, or jugo de lulo, is a staple of Colombian homes, restaurants, and street vendors, offering a burst of freshness that is perfect for combating the country's warm climate.

The preparation of lulo juice is as simple as it is delightful. The fruit is typically sliced open, and its juicy pulp is scooped out and blended with water and a touch of sugar to balance its natural tartness. Some prefer to strain the juice for a smoother texture, while others enjoy it with the pulp intact for a more robust and natural experience. The result is a drink that is not only refreshing but also visually striking, with its vibrant greenish-orange hue and frothy top. Served over ice, lulo juice is a favorite accompaniment to meals, especially in the afternoon when the heat is at its peak.

Beyond its refreshing taste, lulo juice carries cultural and nutritional significance. The fruit is known for its high vitamin

C content and antioxidant properties, making it a popular choice for those seeking a healthy beverage. It is also a symbol of Colombia's natural wealth, representing the country's diverse ecosystems and the fruits that thrive within them. In rural areas, particularly in the Andean region, lulo is often grown in small family farms, where its cultivation supports local communities and preserves traditional agricultural practices.

While aguardiente and lulo juice represent two extremes of Colombia's beverage culture, the rise of Colombian craft beer offers a modern and dynamic addition to the country's drinking scene. Over the past decade, craft breweries have emerged across Colombia, challenging the dominance of mass-produced beers and introducing a new world of flavors to local palates. This movement is driven by a generation of brewers who are passionate about quality, experimentation, and showcasing Colombia's unique ingredients.

Craft breweries in cities like Bogotá, Medellín, and Cali have gained popularity by offering a diverse range of beer styles, from hoppy IPAs and rich stouts to refreshing lagers and fruity ales. Many of these breweries incorporate local ingredients into their recipes, creating beers that are distinctly Colombian. For example, some brewers use panela, an unrefined cane sugar, to add depth and sweetness, while others experiment with tropical fruits like guava, passion fruit, or lulo to create refreshing, fruit-forward brews. These innovations not only set Colombian craft beer apart but also celebrate the country's agricultural heritage.

The craft beer scene has also fostered a sense of community and creativity, with breweries often hosting events, tastings, and collaborations. Taprooms have become gathering places where people can enjoy a pint while learning about the brewing process and the stories behind each beer. This connection between brewers and consumers has helped to cultivate a culture of appreciation for artisanal beer, moving beyond mere consumption to a deeper understanding of the craft. The success of Colombian craft beer has even begun to attract international attention, with some breweries exporting their creations to markets abroad, further elevating the country's reputation as a hub for innovation and quality.

As craft beer gains traction, it also plays a role in redefining Colombia's drinking culture. While traditional beverages like aguardiente and lulo juice remain beloved, the rise of craft beer reflects a growing interest in diversity and experimentation. This shift is particularly evident among younger generations, who are eager to explore new flavors and support local artisans. Craft beer has become a symbol of modern Colombia—dynamic, creative, and deeply connected to its roots.

The diversity of Colombian beverages mirrors the diversity of the country itself, offering a taste of its landscapes, traditions, and innovations with every sip. From the fiery embrace of aguardiente to the cooling tang of lulo juice and the bold creativity of craft beer, each drink tells a story of its own. Whether you're toasting with friends late into the night, sipping on a refreshing juice under the midday sun, or sampling a flight of locally brewed beers, these experiences are an invitation to connect with Colombia's people, culture, and spirit.

What makes these beverages truly remarkable is their ability to bring people together, transcending differences and creating shared moments of joy. They are a reflection of Colombia's warmth and hospitality, its love of celebration, and its deep appreciation for the natural and cultural treasures that define the nation. To savor these drinks is to embrace a piece of Colombia's identity, one that lingers long after the glass is empty.

# CHAPTER 5: ADVENTURE ACTIVITIES AND OUTDOOR EXPERIENCES

## Hiking and Trekking: Discovering Colombia's Trails

Colombia's diverse landscapes provide an unparalleled playground for hiking and trekking enthusiasts, offering trails that weave through lush jungles, misty cloud forests, arid deserts, towering mountain ranges, and even ancient archaeological sites. From the iconic Andes to the remote Amazon basin, the country's natural beauty invites exploration, while its trails reveal the stories of its history, culture, and biodiversity. Hiking in Colombia is more than just a physical challenge—it's an intimate way to connect with its people, landscapes, and past. Whether you're an experienced trekker or a beginner looking to explore, Colombia's trails promise unforgettable adventures.

The Lost City, or Ciudad Perdida, is one of Colombia's most famous trekking destinations and provides an experience that is both physically demanding and culturally enriching. Hidden deep in the Sierra Nevada de Santa Marta mountains, this ancient archaeological site predates Machu Picchu and was once the spiritual and political hub of the Tairona civilization. Reaching the Lost City requires a four- to six-day trek through dense jungle, crossing rivers, climbing steep trails, and navigating humid conditions. Along the way, trekkers pass through indigenous Kogi villages, where locals often share insights into their traditions and the sacred significance of the site. The journey culminates with the awe-inspiring sight of stone terraces and stairways that emerge from the forest—an unforgettable reward for those who make the effort.

The trek to the Lost City is a testament to Colombia's commitment to preserving its cultural heritage while promoting sustainable tourism. Licensed guides, many of whom are from the local indigenous communities, are required for the trek, ensuring that visitors respect the environment and the cultural significance of the site. The experience is as much about the journey as the destination. Nights are spent in rustic campsites, where trekkers bond over shared meals and stories, while the sounds of the jungle provide a natural soundtrack. Despite the physical challenges, the trek is accessible to most with a moderate level of fitness, making it one of Colombia's most rewarding adventures.

For those seeking high-altitude challenges, the Cocuy National Park in the eastern Andes offers some of the most breathtaking landscapes in Colombia. This remote park is home to the Sierra Nevada del Cocuy, a stunning mountain range dotted with snow-capped peaks, glacial lakes, and sweeping valleys. Trekkers can choose from several trails that vary in length and difficulty, with the Laguna Grande de la Sierra trek being a favorite. This trail takes hikers through dramatic terrain to a pristine glacial lake, framed by towering peaks that seem to touch the sky. The park's high-altitude environment requires careful acclimatization, but the effort is rewarded with views that few places on Earth can match.

Cocuy National Park is also a haven for wildlife, with species such as the Andean condor, spectacled bear, and white-tailed deer making their home in the rugged terrain. The park is managed with strict conservation policies, and visitors must hire accredited guides to ensure the trails are respected and preserved. The local U'wa indigenous community plays an active role in protecting the park, adding a layer of cultural depth to the experience. Trekkers are reminded that the mountains are sacred to the U'wa, who view them as living entities deserving of reverence and care. As a result, hiking in Cocuy is not just a physical journey but also an opportunity to engage with Colombia's indigenous perspectives on nature and spirituality.

In contrast to the alpine beauty of Cocuy, the Tatacoa Desert offers a completely different hiking experience. Located in the Huila department, this arid landscape is characterized by its surreal rock formations, red canyons, and labyrinthine trails. Often compared to a Martian landscape, the desert is a photographer's dream, with its dramatic colors and textures shifting throughout the day as the light changes. Hiking in Tatacoa is less about endurance and more about exploration, with trails that lead to hidden oases, fossil beds, and panoramic viewpoints. The desert's clear skies also make it a prime destination for stargazing, adding an extra dimension to the experience.

Tatacoa's unique ecosystem is home to a surprising variety of flora and fauna, including cacti, iguanas, and birds. The trails are relatively easy to navigate, making the desert an accessible option for hikers of all levels. Local guides can provide fascinating insights into the region's geology, history, and folklore, enriching the experience. A hike in Tatacoa is not just an adventure but a step into a world that feels utterly removed from the verdant landscapes typically associated with Colombia. The contrast between the desert's arid beauty and the lushness of other regions underscores the country's incredible diversity.

The Valle de Cocora, located in the Coffee Triangle, is another must-visit destination for hikers. Famous for its towering wax palms—the national tree of Colombia—this valley offers trails that wind through rolling hills, cloud forests, and open meadows. The loop trail to Acaime, a hummingbird sanctuary, is particularly popular, combining moderate difficulty with stunning scenery. As hikers ascend through the forest, they are greeted by the sight of wax palms rising up to 60 meters into the sky, their slender trunks swaying gracefully in the breeze. The valley's beauty is both tranquil and majestic, making it a favorite among nature lovers and photographers.

The Valle de Cocora is also a gateway to Los Nevados National Park, where more challenging hikes await. Trails in the park lead to volcanic peaks such as Nevado del Ruiz and Nevado del Tolima, offering a mix of volcanic landscapes, glacial formations, and high-altitude grasslands known as páramos. These treks require careful preparation and often the assistance of guides, but they provide an unparalleled opportunity to explore one of Colombia's most dramatic natural environments. The páramos, in particular, are unique ecosystems found only in a few places on Earth, and they play a crucial role in regulating Colombia's water supply.

For those who prefer shorter hikes with a cultural twist, the Camino Real in Santander provides a perfect blend of history and scenery. This ancient stone pathway, originally built by the Guane indigenous people and later expanded during colonial times, connects the towns of Barichara and Guane. The trail is relatively easy, taking about two to three hours to complete, and offers stunning views of the surrounding countryside. Along the way, hikers can admire the traditional architecture of Barichara, often called the most beautiful town in Colombia, as well as the charming village of Guane, known for its small museums and artisanal crafts.

Hiking in Colombia is not without its challenges, and preparation is key to ensuring a safe and enjoyable experience. The country's varied climates mean that hikers should be ready for everything from intense heat in the lowlands to freezing temperatures in the high Andes. Proper footwear, layered clothing, and plenty of water are essential, as is sunscreen and insect repellent. Hiring local guides is often recommended, not only for safety but also for the invaluable knowledge they bring. Guides can provide insights into the flora, fauna, and history of the trails, transforming a hike into an educational journey.

Colombia's trails also carry a sense of responsibility. Many of the landscapes you'll encounter are fragile ecosystems that require careful stewardship. Visitors are encouraged to practice Leave No Trace principles, respecting the environment and minimizing their impact. This includes sticking to marked trails, avoiding littering, and being mindful of the wildlife. By treading lightly, hikers can help ensure that Colombia's natural beauty remains intact for future generations to enjoy.

The joy of hiking in Colombia lies not only in the physical act of walking but also in the connections it fosters—to the land, to its people, and to oneself. Each trail offers a unique perspective on the country, revealing layers of history, culture, and natural wonder that are impossible to experience any other way. Whether you're standing among the ancient terraces of the Lost City, gazing at the stars in the Tatacoa Desert, or feeling the mist of a cloud forest in Cocora, Colombia's trails offer moments of awe and discovery that linger long after the journey ends.

## Scuba Diving and Snorkeling in Caribbean Waters

The Caribbean waters off the coast of Colombia are a dazzling haven for scuba diving and snorkeling enthusiasts, offering some of the most pristine and biodiverse marine environments in the world. With coral reefs that teem with life, sunken shipwrecks steeped in history, and crystal-clear waters that range from aquamarine to deep sapphire, the underwater landscapes are as mesmerizing as the country's vibrant terrestrial terrain. From the islands of San Andrés and Providencia to the Rosario Islands and Tayrona National Park, the Colombian Caribbean is a treasure trove for adventurers seeking to explore the mysteries beneath the surface.

San Andrés, located approximately 750 kilometers northwest of mainland Colombia, is perhaps the most renowned destination for underwater exploration in the country. This small island, part of an archipelago that also includes Providencia and Santa Catalina, is surrounded by the UNESCO-designated Seaflower Biosphere Reserve, one of the largest marine protected areas in the Caribbean. The waters here are a kaleidoscope of blues, and the reefs are home to an astonishing variety of marine life, from colorful parrotfish and angelfish to graceful sea turtles and stingrays. San Andrés is celebrated for its visibility, which often exceeds 30 meters, making it an ideal spot for both novice and experienced divers.

The dive sites around San Andrés are incredibly diverse, catering to different levels of experience and interests. One of the most popular spots is El Acuario, a shallow area perfect for snorkeling, where the water is so clear that you can see schools of fish darting between the coral formations from the surface. For scuba divers, the Blue Hole offers a dramatic descent into a cavernous space surrounded by coral walls that attract an array of sea creatures. Another highlight is La Pirámide, a submerged coral formation that resembles a pyramid and is frequented by barracudas and eagle rays. These sites are not just about the marine life; they also showcase the vibrant health of the coral reefs, which come in shades of pink, orange, and purple.

Providencia, the quieter and less developed sibling of San Andrés, is a hidden gem for those seeking a more tranquil diving experience. The island's reefs are less crowded and boast an exceptional level of biodiversity. The famed Crab Cay, or Cayo Cangrejo, is a must-visit spot for snorkelers, with its shallow waters and thriving coral gardens. Scuba divers often head to the nearby site known as Felipe's Place, where they can encounter nurse sharks, moray eels, and massive schools of jackfish. The waters around Providencia are also home to larger pelagic species such as reef sharks and, occasionally, hammerheads, providing thrilling encounters for more experienced divers.

What sets Providencia apart is its commitment to sustainable tourism. The local community has worked tirelessly to preserve the island's natural beauty and marine ecosystems, implementing strict regulations on fishing and diving activities. This emphasis on conservation ensures that the reefs remain vibrant and healthy, offering visitors an unspoiled glimpse into the underwater world. The pace of life on Providencia is slower, and the diving experience reflects this, allowing for a more intimate connection with the marine environment.

Closer to mainland Colombia, the Rosario Islands, located just off the coast of Cartagena, present another fantastic destination for underwater exploration. This archipelago, part of the Rosario and San Bernardo Corals National Natural Park, is known for its coral reefs that flourish in shallow waters, making it particularly appealing for snorkelers. The vibrant underwater scene includes brain coral, sea fans, and sponges that create a kaleidoscopic backdrop for the schools of fish that dart through the currents. The park's protected status has helped to maintain the health of the reefs, despite their proximity to the bustling city of Cartagena.

One of the most accessible snorkeling spots in the Rosario Islands is Isla Grande, where shallow reefs allow even beginners to experience the beauty of the marine world. Snorkelers can expect to see sergeant majors, butterflyfish, and damselfish, as well as the occasional octopus hiding among the crevices. For scuba divers, the sunken wreck of a small cargo ship near Isla Barú provides an eerie yet fascinating site to explore, with coral and sponges gradually reclaiming the structure and turning it into a haven for marine life. Night dives in this area reveal bioluminescent plankton that light up the water like stars, creating a magical and unforgettable experience.

Tayrona National Park, located on Colombia's northern coast near Santa Marta, offers a unique blend of lush jungle and turquoise waters, making it a favorite destination for nature lovers. While the park is best known for its stunning beaches and hiking trails, its underwater treasures are equally impressive. The coral reefs here are less extensive than those in San Andrés or the Rosario Islands, but they are no less captivating. Snorkeling at La Piscina, a calm, sheltered bay, reveals a vibrant underwater world filled with colorful fish, sea urchins, and starfish. The clear, shallow waters make it an ideal spot for families and beginners.

For scuba divers, deeper excursions in Tayrona's waters uncover a world of volcanic rock formations and coral outcrops. Sites like Granate and Punta Aguja offer a mix of hard and soft corals, as well as encounters with barracudas, pufferfish, and even the occasional sea turtle. The park's proximity to the Sierra Nevada de Santa Marta, the world's highest coastal mountain range, creates a dramatic backdrop for underwater adventures. It's a place where the mountains meet the sea, and every dive feels like a journey into a hidden realm.

Colombia's Caribbean waters are not just about reefs and fish; they also hold a wealth of history beneath their surface. The region is dotted with shipwrecks, remnants of Colombia's colonial past and the battles fought over its treasures. These wrecks are now artificial reefs, providing shelter for marine life and intriguing sites for divers. Off the coast of Cartagena, the remains of Spanish galleons lie scattered on the seabed, attracting both history buffs and diving enthusiasts. Exploring these wrecks is like stepping back in time, with cannons and anchors encrusted in coral serving as reminders of a bygone era.

Safety and sustainability are central to the diving and snorkeling experience in Colombia. Many operators are committed to protecting the marine environment, offering eco-friendly tours and educating visitors on responsible practices. Divers and snorkelers are encouraged to respect the reefs by avoiding touching the coral and maintaining a safe distance from marine life. These efforts are vital in preserving the health of Colombia's underwater ecosystems, ensuring that future generations can enjoy their beauty.

The accessibility of Colombia's Caribbean waters makes them ideal for divers and snorkelers of all levels. Beginners can take advantage of calm, shallow sites with excellent visibility, while advanced divers can challenge themselves with deep walls, drift dives, and encounters with larger marine species. Many dive shops and schools offer certification courses, allowing newcomers to gain the skills and confidence needed to explore the underwater world. The sense of accomplishment that comes with completing a dive or snorkeling excursion is matched only by the awe inspired by the vibrant marine life and the serenity of the ocean.

Exploring Colombia's underwater landscapes is a journey of discovery, one that reveals the intricate connections between land, sea, and culture. Each dive or snorkeling trip offers a new perspective, whether it's the vibrant colors of a coral reef, the graceful movements of a manta ray, or the haunting beauty of a sunken ship. The experience is not just about what you see but also about how it makes you feel—a sense of wonder, respect, and connection to the natural world.

Colombia's Caribbean waters are a testament to the country's incredible biodiversity and its commitment to preserving these natural treasures. From the bustling reefs of San Andrés to the tranquil bays of Tayrona, each destination offers its own unique charm and challenges. Whether you're floating above a shallow reef, descending into the depths of a blue hole, or exploring the history hidden in a shipwreck, the experience is one that stays with you long after you return to the surface. It's a reminder of the beauty and mystery of the ocean and the importance of protecting it for generations to come.

## Paragliding Over the Chicamocha Canyon

The Chicamocha Canyon, one of Colombia's most breathtaking natural wonders, offers an experience that is as thrilling as it is awe-inspiring: paragliding over its vast, dramatic expanse. Located in the department of Santander, near the vibrant city of Bucaramanga, the canyon is a geological marvel that cuts through the Andes, stretching for over 200 kilometers and plunging to depths of 2,000 meters. Its rugged terrain, carved over millennia by the Chicamocha River, has created a landscape of towering cliffs, winding valleys, and striking contrasts of color. But while its beauty is undeniable from below, it is from above, soaring through the open skies, that the canyon's true majesty is revealed. Paragliding over the Chicamocha Canyon offers not only an adrenaline rush but also a rare perspective on one of the most extraordinary natural environments in the world.

The journey to Chicamocha begins with a drive through the picturesque Santander countryside, where rolling hills and quaint villages set the stage for the adventure ahead. The region's rugged beauty is a prelude to the grandeur of the canyon itself, which seems to appear suddenly as the road winds closer. The first glimpse of the canyon is often enough to leave visitors speechless—its sheer scale and depth are humbling, a testament to the power of nature. Perched on the edge of this immense landscape are several paragliding launch sites, strategically chosen for their elevation and wind conditions. These sites are managed by experienced operators who prioritize safety and ensure that every flight is as smooth and enjoyable as possible.

For those new to paragliding, the experience can be both exhilarating and intimidating. The thought of running off the edge of a cliff, even while securely harnessed to an experienced pilot, requires a leap of faith—both figuratively and literally. Tandem flights, the most common option for beginners, pair visitors with professional pilots who handle all the technical aspects of the flight. After a thorough briefing on safety procedures and what to expect, participants are fitted with a harness and helmet before being secured to the pilot. The launch itself is surprisingly simple: a few steps forward, a gust of wind catching the sail, and suddenly, the ground falls away as you're lifted into the air. The sensation is both surreal and liberating, a mix of weightlessness and exhilaration as the canopy carries you upward.

From the moment you leave the ground, the perspective shifts dramatically. The canyon, which seemed immense from its rim, becomes an endless tapestry of textures and colors as you glide above it. The jagged cliffs, lined with layers of sediment that tell the story of millions of years, contrast with the smooth curves of the river far below. Vegetation clings to the canyon walls in patches of green, while the river glimmers in the sunlight like a silver thread weaving through the landscape. The air is crisp and cool at higher altitudes, and the only sounds are the rustle of the wind and the occasional instructions from your pilot, who points out landmarks and adjusts the flight path for optimal views.

The Chicamocha Canyon's unique microclimate makes it an ideal location for paragliding almost year-round. The winds that sweep through the canyon create stable thermals, or columns of rising air, which pilots use to gain altitude and extend the duration of the flight. These thermals are key to the experience, allowing for a leisurely exploration of the canyon's vast expanse rather than a rapid descent. Depending on the weather and the skill of the pilot, flights can last anywhere from 15 to 40 minutes, during which time the scenery constantly evolves. One moment you might be circling above a sheer cliff face, the next you're drifting over a patch of farmland or skimming the edge of a ridge.

For the adventurous, some pilots offer the option of adding acrobatic maneuvers to the flight. These include spins, dives, and other dramatic moves that amplify the adrenaline rush and showcase the pilot's skill. While these maneuvers are entirely optional and not for the faint of heart, they add an extra layer of excitement for those seeking a truly unforgettable experience. Even without the acrobatics, the sheer act of flying—of defying gravity and moving with the currents of the wind—is an adventure unlike any other.

The Chicamocha Canyon is more than just a backdrop for paragliding; it is a living, breathing ecosystem steeped in history and culture. The canyon is home to a variety of plant and animal species, some of which are endemic to the region. From the air, it's possible to spot birds of prey like hawks and vultures riding the same thermals as your paraglider, their graceful movements a reminder of the natural harmony that exists here. The canyon also holds deep cultural significance, as it was once home to the Guane people, an indigenous group whose legacy is preserved in the artifacts and petroglyphs found throughout the area.

After landing, which is typically a smooth descent onto a designated field or open area, the sense of accomplishment and exhilaration is palpable. Many describe the experience as transformative, a moment of pure freedom and connection to nature. The pilots and operators often share in this joy, as their passion for flight and the canyon is evident in their enthusiasm and knowledge. For those who wish to relive the experience, many operators offer the option to purchase photos or videos taken during the flight, captured by cameras mounted on the paraglider's harness.

While paragliding is undoubtedly the highlight for many visitors to Chicamocha, the area offers much more to explore. The Chicamocha National Park, also known as Panachi, is a popular destination that complements the aerial adventure with land-based activities. The park features hiking trails, cable car rides, and viewpoints that offer stunning vistas of the canyon from different angles. Its facilities include restaurants and shops where visitors can sample local Santander cuisine or purchase handicrafts as souvenirs. The park's cable car, one of the longest in the world, provides an alternative way to experience the canyon's scale, gliding over its depths in a more relaxed manner.

For those who wish to extend their stay, the nearby town of San Gil serves as a hub for outdoor activities and adventure tourism. Known as the adventure capital of Colombia, San Gil offers opportunities for rafting, caving, and mountain biking, making it an excellent base for exploring the region. The town itself is charming, with cobblestone streets, colonial architecture, and a lively central plaza where locals and visitors gather. From San Gil, it's also possible to visit Barichara, often called the most beautiful town in Colombia, which provides a tranquil counterpoint to the adrenaline-fueled adventures of Chicamocha.

Safety is a top priority in paragliding, and Colombia's operators adhere to strict standards to ensure that every flight is conducted responsibly. Equipment is regularly inspected and maintained, and pilots are highly trained and certified. Visitors are encouraged to follow all instructions provided by their guides and to disclose any medical conditions that might affect their ability to participate. While the activity carries inherent risks, these precautions minimize them, allowing participants to focus on the experience without undue worry.

Paragliding over the Chicamocha Canyon is more than just an adventure; it's a way to see Colombia from a perspective that few ever get to experience. The combination of natural beauty, adrenaline, and serenity is unparalleled, creating memories that last a lifetime. Whether you're a thrill-seeker looking for your next challenge or a traveler eager to connect with the landscape in a profound way, this experience offers something truly special. The canyon's vastness, its intricate details, and the sense of freedom that comes with flight all combine to make it one of Colombia's most unforgettable experiences.

## Whitewater Rafting and Kayaking on Colombia's Rivers

Colombia's rivers are lifelines that carve through its lush landscapes, connecting dense jungles, vast savannas, and towering mountains. These waterways are not only vital for the communities that reside along their banks but also serve as exhilarating playgrounds for adventure seekers. Whitewater rafting and kayaking in Colombia offer thrills that range from heart-pounding rapids to peaceful stretches where paddlers can immerse themselves in the surrounding scenery. With rivers flowing through some of the most biodiverse regions in the world, these adventures are as much about connecting with nature as they are about testing your courage and skill. From the Magdalena and Cauca rivers to the more remote and untamed waters of the Guaviare and Fonce, Colombia's rivers promise unforgettable experiences for both beginners and seasoned paddlers.

The Fonce River in the department of Santander is one of the most popular destinations for whitewater rafting in Colombia. Flowing through the adventure capital of San Gil, the Fonce delivers a mix of rapids that are ideal for both novices and experienced rafters. Its Class II and III rapids provide plenty of excitement without being overly technical, making it a perfect introduction for beginners. For those who have never set foot in a raft, San Gil's many adventure tour operators offer guided trips that include safety briefings, equipment rentals, and experienced guides who ensure a safe and thrilling ride. The Fonce River is not just about the rapids, though; its lush surroundings and clear waters create an atmosphere of natural beauty that enhances the entire experience. Between rapids, there are moments of calm where you can take in the scenery, spot wildlife along the banks, or simply enjoy the camaraderie of your fellow paddlers.

Santander's rivers have long been central to the lives of local communities, and rafting on the Fonce offers a chance to connect with this heritage. Many of the guides are locals who grew up by the river and know its every twist and turn. Their knowledge goes beyond navigation; they share stories about the region's history, its flora and fauna, and the deep cultural ties that bind the people to the water. This connection adds a layer of richness to the experience, turning a day of rafting into a deeper exploration of Colombian life.

For those seeking a greater challenge, the Suarez River, also located near San Gil, is a step up in intensity and adventure. Known for its powerful Class IV and V rapids, the Suarez is not for the faint of heart. Its churning waters and steep drops demand a high level of skill and teamwork, making it best suited for experienced rafters or those looking to push their limits. The adrenaline rush of navigating these rapids is unparalleled, with every twist and surge of the river demanding focus and precision. Between the bursts of whitewater, the river offers glimpses of Santander's rugged beauty, with steep canyon walls and verdant hills forming a dramatic backdrop to the adventure.

Guided excursions on the Suarez River are meticulously planned, with safety as the top priority. Before setting off, participants receive thorough training on paddling techniques, communication signals, and how to handle unexpected situations. Guides lead the way, steering the rafts through the most challenging sections and ensuring that everyone works together as a cohesive team. The experience is as much about trust and collaboration as it is about individual skill, with each successful run through a rapid bringing a surge of collective triumph.

Colombia's rivers are not limited to Santander. The Magdalena River, the country's longest and most iconic waterway, offers its own unique opportunities for paddlers.

While much of the lower Magdalena is calm and navigable by larger boats, the upper stretches near Huila and Tolima are home to rapids that attract kayakers and rafters. The Magdalena River winds through a landscape of Andean foothills, coffee plantations, and dense forests, creating a scenic backdrop for paddling adventures. The river's rapids vary in difficulty, providing options for paddlers of all experience levels. In calmer sections, kayakers can take their time exploring hidden coves and spotting birds, monkeys, and other wildlife that thrive along the riverbanks.

The Magdalena River holds immense historical and cultural significance for Colombia, having served as a vital trade route and source of sustenance for centuries. Paddling its waters is a journey through this history, with the surrounding landscapes often dotted with remnants of colonial towns, ancient petroglyphs, and traditional fishing communities. Local guides enrich the experience by sharing stories of the river's role in Colombian folklore and daily life, adding depth to the adventure. The Magdalena is not just a river; it is a living testament to the country's past and present, and exploring it by kayak or raft offers a connection to this legacy.

In the heart of the Amazon basin, the Guaviare River presents one of Colombia's most remote and untamed paddling experiences. This mighty river flows through dense rainforest, offering paddlers the chance to immerse themselves in one of the world's most biodiverse ecosystems. The Guaviare is less about adrenaline-pumping rapids and more about the sheer wonder of its surroundings. Kayaking or rafting here is a journey into the wild, where you can encounter pink river dolphins, caimans, and countless species of birds. The river's calm stretches are perfect for absorbing the sounds and sights of the jungle, while its occasional rapids provide just enough excitement to keep things interesting.

The Guaviare River is also a gateway to some of Colombia's most fascinating natural and cultural treasures. Nearby, the Serranía de la Lindosa is home to ancient rock art that dates back thousands of years, depicting scenes of animals, humans, and spiritual practices. Many paddling excursions on the

Guaviare combine river exploration with visits to these archaeological sites, creating a holistic adventure that blends nature, history, and culture. Navigating this river feels like stepping back in time, with every bend revealing something new and awe-inspiring.

Kayaking enthusiasts will also find plenty to love in Colombia, where the country's varied rivers offer opportunities for everything from leisurely paddles to technical whitewater challenges. The Cauca River, running parallel to the Andes, is a favorite for kayakers seeking a mix of scenery and moderate rapids. Its waters flow through a landscape of fertile valleys and towering peaks, with sections that cater to both beginners and more experienced paddlers. Kayaking on the Cauca is a chance to connect with Colombia's agricultural heartland, as the river irrigates fields of sugarcane, coffee, and other crops that sustain local communities.

Safety and preparation are integral to any rafting or kayaking adventure in Colombia. While the thrill of navigating rapids is undeniably appealing, it's essential to approach these activities with the proper precautions. Most operators provide all necessary equipment, including helmets, life jackets, and paddles, and adhere to strict safety standards. Participants should ensure they are physically capable of handling the demands of the river and follow all instructions from their guides. Hydration, sunscreen, and appropriate clothing are also important, as the combination of physical exertion and exposure to the elements can be taxing.

The environmental importance of Colombia's rivers cannot be overstated, and efforts to preserve these waterways are critical. Many of the regions where rafting and kayaking take place are home to delicate ecosystems that rely on the health of the rivers to thrive. Eco-conscious operators are increasingly adopting sustainable practices, such as minimizing waste, using eco-friendly equipment, and educating participants about the importance of conservation. By respecting the rivers and their surroundings, paddlers can contribute to the ongoing efforts to protect these invaluable natural resources.

Whitewater rafting and kayaking in Colombia offer more than just adventure; they provide a unique way to explore the country's landscapes, connect with its people, and appreciate the natural forces that have shaped its geography and culture. Each river tells its own story, from the tranquil beauty of the Guaviare to the roaring rapids of the Suarez, and each adventure leaves participants with memories that go far beyond the thrill of the ride. Whether you're navigating the twists and turns of a challenging rapid or gliding through a calm stretch of jungle-fringed water, the experience is one of discovery, challenge, and connection. Colombia's rivers are not just destinations; they are journeys, inviting you to dive into their depths and emerge with a greater understanding of the world around you.

## Birdwatching: Exploring the World's Most Diverse Avian Life

Colombia is a paradise for birdwatchers, boasting more bird species than any other country in the world. With a recorded 1,966 species, which accounts for nearly 20% of the planet's bird diversity, the country is a magnet for ornithologists, naturalists, and travelers seeking to immerse themselves in its unparalleled avian richness. Stretching from the Amazon rainforest to the Andes, from the Pacific coast to the Caribbean lowlands, Colombia's diverse ecosystems provide habitats for a staggering variety of species, including some of the rarest and most colorful birds on Earth. Whether you're an experienced birder or a curious beginner, Colombia offers the chance to witness an extraordinary array of feathered life in settings as awe-inspiring as the birds themselves.

The Andes, with their dramatic elevations and lush cloud forests, are one of the most prominent regions for birdwatching in Colombia. This mountain range, which splits into three branches as it runs through the country, creates an abundance of microclimates and habitats, each supporting unique bird populations. Among the most sought-after species in the Andes are the brightly colored tanagers, toucanets, and hummingbirds. The Andean Cock-of-the-Rock, with its brilliant orange plumage and flamboyant courtship displays, is a highlight for many birders. Its leks, or communal mating grounds, are often found in forested areas near streams, and witnessing these birds perform their elaborate dances is an unforgettable experience.

Mindo Loma and Jardin, two picturesque towns nestled in the Andes, are prime birding destinations. In Mindo Loma, feeders attract dozens of hummingbird species, including the striking Sword-billed Hummingbird, whose beak is longer than its body—a marvel of evolution adapted for feeding on deep tubular flowers. In Jardin, the Yellow-eared Parrot, a critically endangered species, can often be spotted around wax palms, its preferred nesting site. The preservation of wax palms is essential for the survival of this parrot, and efforts to conserve both the trees and the birds have made Jardin a symbol of successful conservation practices.

The Magdalena Valley, which stretches between the Central and Eastern Andes, serves as another crucial birding hotspot. This region is home to species such as the White-mantled Barbet, a striking black-and-white bird with a bright red face, and the Sooty Ant-Tanager, a bird found only in Colombia. The Magdalena River, which runs through the valley, provides vital wetlands that attract waterfowl, herons, and migratory birds. Exploring the valley's reserves and riverbanks offers birdwatchers access to rare species that thrive in its unique environment.

Colombia's Amazon rainforest, a sprawling expanse of dense vegetation and waterways, holds an entirely different set of avian treasures. The Amazon is one of the most biodiverse regions on Earth, and its birdlife reflects this richness. Toucans, macaws, and parrots are some of the most iconic species found here, their vibrant plumage standing out against the emerald backdrop of the jungle. Early morning excursions by boat or on foot often reward birders with sightings of mixed-species flocks, where dozens of birds of different species move together through the canopy. These flocks are a testament to the interconnectedness of Amazonian ecosystems, with species relying on one another for protection and foraging efficiency.

In the Amazon, the Hoatzin—a peculiar, prehistoric-looking bird—is a must-see. Known locally as the "stinkbird" due to the fermented odor of its diet, the Hoatzin is unique in its biology and behavior. It feeds almost exclusively on leaves and possesses a digestive system more akin to that of a cow than a bird. Watching a Hoatzin perch near a waterway, its spiky crest and awkward movements adding to its charm, is a reminder of the strange and wonderful diversity of life in the Amazon.

The Pacific coast of Colombia, particularly the Chocó region, is another essential destination for birdwatchers. This area is one of the wettest places on Earth, with rainforests that teem with biodiversity. The Chocó is home to endemic species such as the Long-wattled Umbrellabird, whose males display an extraordinary feathered "wattle" during courtship rituals. The region's rivers and mangroves attract kingfishers, herons, and egrets, while the forests echo with the calls of antbirds and manakins. Birding in the Chocó often involves navigating dense vegetation and dealing with high humidity, but the rewards are well worth the effort.

The Sierra Nevada de Santa Marta, an isolated mountain range on Colombia's northern coast, is considered one of the most important sites for bird conservation in the world. This region is home to 36 endemic bird species, many of which are found nowhere else on the planet. The Santa Marta Parakeet, the Santa Marta Antpitta, and the Santa Marta Screech-Owl are just a few of the rare and fascinating species that draw birdwatchers to this area. The range's elevation gradient creates a variety of habitats, from tropical forests at its base to páramo grasslands near its peaks, each hosting a distinct set of avian species.

The Caribbean coast, with its wetlands, mangroves, and dry forests, offers yet another dimension to Colombia's birding opportunities. The Los Flamencos Sanctuary, located near the town of Riohacha, is famous for its population of American

Flamingos, which wade gracefully through the shallow lagoons. The sanctuary is also home to a wide range of shorebirds, herons, and pelicans. Nearby, the dry forests of the Guajira Peninsula are inhabited by species such as the Vermilion Cardinal, a striking red bird that contrasts vividly with the arid landscape.

Migratory birds add another layer of excitement to birdwatching in Colombia. The country serves as a critical stopover point for species traveling along the Americas flyway, with thousands of birds passing through each year. Raptors, warblers, and shorebirds can be seen during migration seasons, adding a dynamic element to the birding calendar. Certain locations, such as the wetlands around Bogotá, become temporary homes for migratory species, providing birdwatchers with opportunities to see birds that are only present for a few months.

Birdwatching in Colombia is not just about the birds; it's also about the people and communities who are deeply connected to these environments. Many local guides are avid birders themselves, with an intimate knowledge of the habitats and behaviors of the species in their region. These guides enhance the birding experience by sharing their expertise and passion, often leading visitors to hidden spots where elusive birds can be found. Community-based conservation initiatives, such as those in the Sierra Nevada de Santa Marta and the Amazon, demonstrate how protecting birds can also benefit local people, creating sustainable livelihoods and fostering a sense of pride in Colombia's natural heritage.

Preparation is key for anyone planning a birdwatching trip in Colombia. A good pair of binoculars, a field guide specific to Colombian birds, and comfortable clothing suitable for the climate are essential. Many birding tours and lodges cater specifically to enthusiasts, offering amenities such as observation towers, feeding stations, and expert-led excursions. Patience and a keen eye are invaluable, as some species require careful observation to spot. Early mornings are often the best time for birding, as this is when many birds are most active and vocal.

Colombia's remarkable bird diversity is a reflection of its varied landscapes, but it also underscores the importance of conservation. Habitat destruction, climate change, and illegal wildlife trade pose significant threats to many species. However, efforts to protect Colombia's birds are gaining momentum, with national parks, reserves, and community-led initiatives playing critical roles in preserving habitats. Birdwatchers contribute to these efforts by supporting ecotourism and raising awareness of the need to protect these natural treasures.

Exploring Colombia's birdlife is a journey into the heart of one of the most biodiverse countries on Earth. Each region reveals a different facet of the avian world, from the dazzling colors of tanagers in the Andes to the haunting calls of owls in the Santa Marta mountains. The experience is one of constant discovery, with every sighting bringing a sense of wonder and connection to the natural world. For anyone with a love of birds, Colombia is a destination that offers not only unparalleled diversity but also the chance to be part of a global effort to celebrate and protect these extraordinary creatures.

## Cycling and Mountain Biking Across Colombia's Landscapes

Colombia's diverse and dramatic terrain makes it a cyclist's dream come true, with routes that cater to every kind of rider, from road cyclists seeking steep mountain ascents to mountain bikers eager to tackle rugged trails through rainforests and deserts. The country's varied landscapes—spanning the towering Andes, rolling coffee plantations, dense Amazonian jungles, and arid plains—offer countless opportunities for exploration on two wheels. Cycling in Colombia isn't just about the challenge or the thrill; it's about immersing yourself in the country's culture, connecting with its people, and experiencing its breathtaking natural beauty from an intimate vantage point. For beginners and seasoned riders alike, Colombia's roads and trails promise unforgettable adventures.

The Andes mountains dominate Colombia's topography and provide some of the most iconic cycling routes in the country. These steep and winding roads have become a rite of passage for cyclists, as they include legendary climbs that have tested even the world's top athletes in professional races like the Vuelta a Colombia and international events. Routes such as Alto de Letras, often referred to as one of the longest climbs in the world, are a testament to the endurance and determination required to conquer the Andean heights. Stretching for over 80 kilometers and climbing nearly 3,800 meters in elevation, the journey from the town of Mariquita to the summit is both a physical and mental challenge. Riders are rewarded not only with a sense of accomplishment but also with sweeping views of lush valleys, mist-covered peaks, and the occasional glimpse of snow-capped volcanoes.

Road cycling through the Andes can be grueling, but it's also deeply rewarding. Along the way, cyclists pass through small villages where locals often cheer them on, offering smiles, words of encouragement, and sometimes even snacks or a warm cup of coffee. The Andean communities have a deep respect for cyclists, as the sport holds a special place in Colombian culture. Many of the country's most celebrated athletes, like Nairo Quintana and Egan Bernal, hail from these mountainous regions, and their stories inspire countless riders to push their limits on the same roads that shaped these champions.

In contrast to the towering climbs of the Andes, the Coffee Triangle offers a gentler but equally captivating cycling experience. This region, known as the Eje Cafetero, is a UNESCO World Heritage site and one of the most picturesque areas in Colombia. Its rolling hills are draped in emerald-green coffee plantations, dotted with traditional haciendas, and crisscrossed by well-maintained roads and trails. Cycling through the Coffee Triangle is a sensory journey, where the scent of freshly roasted coffee mingles with the crisp mountain air and the sound of birdsong accompanies your ride.

The towns of Salento, Manizales, and Pereira serve as excellent starting points for cycling tours in the Coffee

Triangle. Quiet backroads wind through the countryside, taking riders past coffee farms, rivers, and forests. Some routes lead to hidden waterfalls or natural hot springs, offering refreshing stops along the way. For mountain bikers, the region's trails provide plenty of opportunities to venture off-road, with paths that snake through bamboo groves and traverse rugged terrain. Many local tour operators offer guided rides that include visits to coffee farms, where cyclists can learn about the cultivation and processing of Colombia's most famous export while enjoying a freshly brewed cup of java.

For mountain biking enthusiasts, Colombia's terrain is a playground of technical trails and natural obstacles. The rugged landscapes of Boyacá and Santander are particularly popular among mountain bikers, offering everything from rocky descents to flowing singletrack. In Boyacá, the Iguaque National Park features trails that climb through páramo ecosystems—high-altitude grasslands unique to the Andes. These routes challenge riders with steep ascents and unpredictable weather but reward them with stunning views of glacial lagoons and expansive valleys.

Santander, often called Colombia's adventure capital, is another hotspot for mountain biking. The Chicamocha Canyon, one of the largest canyons in the world, boasts trails that test both skill and stamina. Riders can navigate rocky paths that hug the canyon's edge, descend into its depths on adrenaline-fueled downhill runs, or explore its surrounding countryside on more relaxed routes. The canyon's arid terrain, marked by cacti and rugged cliffs, is a stark contrast to the lush greenery of the Andes, showcasing Colombia's remarkable diversity.

The Tatacoa Desert, located in the Huila department, offers yet another unique cycling experience. This arid region, famous for its surreal red and gray rock formations, is best explored during the cooler hours of the morning or late afternoon. Cycling through the Tatacoa feels like riding on another planet, with its labyrinthine canyons and stark landscapes providing a dramatic backdrop. The lack of vegetation and shade makes this a challenging environment, but the otherworldly beauty and the opportunity to spot unique wildlife, such as iguanas and owls, make it a worthwhile adventure.

Colombia's Caribbean coast offers a more relaxed cycling experience, with flat coastal roads and scenic trails that run alongside golden beaches and turquoise waters. The region around Santa Marta, including the entrance to Tayrona National Park, is particularly popular with cyclists. Here, rides often combine coastal scenery with lush jungle paths, offering glimpses of the Sierra Nevada de Santa Marta mountains in the distance. The coastal breeze and the sound of crashing waves add to the appeal, making this region ideal for riders seeking a more leisurely pace.

Preparation is key for cycling and mountain biking in Colombia, as the country's varied terrain and conditions can present unique challenges. Proper gear, including a reliable bike suited to the terrain, is essential. For road cycling, lightweight bikes with multiple gears are necessary to handle the steep climbs and descents of the Andes. Mountain bikers should opt for bikes with sturdy frames, suspension, and wider tires to tackle rocky trails and uneven surfaces. Clothing should be appropriate for the climate, with layers that can be added or removed as temperatures fluctuate. Sunscreen, hydration packs, and first-aid kits are also crucial, especially for longer rides in remote areas.

Hiring a local guide or joining an organized tour can greatly enhance the experience, particularly for those unfamiliar with the region. Guides not only ensure safety but also provide invaluable insights into the local culture, history, and environment. Many tours include support vehicles that carry supplies and offer assistance in case of mechanical issues, allowing riders to focus on the journey without worrying about logistics. Local guides are also adept at tailoring routes to match the skill level and interests of their groups, ensuring that everyone has an enjoyable and rewarding experience.

Cycling in Colombia is as much about the people as it is about the landscapes. The warmth and hospitality of Colombians are evident at every turn, whether it's a farmer waving from a field, a shopkeeper offering a cold drink, or a fellow cyclist striking up a conversation on the roadside. The country's cycling culture is deeply ingrained, with cycling clubs, races, and events bringing communities together and celebrating the joy of riding. For visitors, joining a local ride or simply sharing the road with Colombian cyclists is a chance to connect with this vibrant culture.

Environmental awareness is an important aspect of cycling in Colombia, as many of the country's trails and routes pass through fragile ecosystems. Cyclists are encouraged to practice Leave No Trace principles, staying on designated paths, avoiding littering, and respecting wildlife. Supporting eco-friendly tour operators and local businesses also contributes to the sustainability of cycling tourism, ensuring that these routes remain accessible and pristine for future generations.

Exploring Colombia on two wheels is a journey of discovery, one that reveals the country's incredible diversity and beauty at every turn. Each region offers a distinct experience, from the challenging climbs of the Andes to the tranquil trails of the Coffee Triangle, the dramatic landscapes of the Tatacoa Desert, and the coastal charm of the Caribbean. Whether you're chasing adrenaline on a rugged mountain trail or savoring the serenity of a quiet countryside ride, cycling in Colombia is an invitation to connect with its land, culture, and spirit in a profound and personal way.

# CHAPTER 6: HIDDEN GEMS AND OFF-THE-BEATEN-PATH DESTINATIONS

## San Agustín Archaeological Park: Ancient Statues and Mysteries

San Agustín Archaeological Park, nestled in the lush hills of Colombia's Huila department, is one of the country's most enigmatic and astonishing cultural treasures. This UNESCO World Heritage Site is home to the largest collection of religious sculptures and megalithic monuments in South America, offering a rare glimpse into the artistry, spirituality, and ingenuity of an ancient civilization. Shrouded in mystery, the people who created these statues left behind no written records, and much about their lives, beliefs, and society remains unknown. What they did leave, however, is a vast array of stone carvings that speak of their profound connection to the spiritual world, their reverence for the dead, and their mastery of artistic expression. Exploring San Agustín Archaeological Park is not just a journey through history—it's an invitation to immerse yourself in the mysteries of one of the most fascinating cultures of pre-Columbian America.

The journey to San Agustín begins with a scenic drive through Colombia's Andean highlands, where rolling hills, coffee plantations, and cloud forests create a stunning backdrop. The park is located about 520 kilometers southwest of Bogotá, and while the trip requires some planning, the reward is well worth the effort. As you approach the town of San Agustín, the landscape shifts to reveal verdant valleys carved by the Magdalena River, Colombia's most important waterway. This region has long been considered sacred, and its natural beauty only adds to the sense of awe that awaits visitors.

Stepping into the park itself is like entering another world. The site spans over 116 hectares and includes more than 500 statues, burial mounds, and ceremonial structures, all of which were crafted between the 1st and 8th centuries CE. The sculptures are scattered across several zones, with the principal areas being the Mesitas (A, B, C, and D), the Fuente de Lavapatas, and the Bosque de las Estatuas. Each of these areas offers a unique perspective on the artistic and spiritual achievements of the San Agustín culture, creating a tapestry of stone and mystery that captivates the imagination.

The Mesitas are the heart of the archaeological park, where visitors can explore burial mounds and ceremonial platforms adorned with intricately carved statues. These statues, often depicting human figures, animals, and mythological creatures, are believed to have guarded tombs and sacred spaces. Many of the carvings exhibit a striking blend of realism and abstraction, with exaggerated features such as large eyes, fanged mouths, and animalistic attributes that suggest a connection to shamanic rituals and spiritual transformation. One of the most famous statues, known as the Double Self, portrays a figure with two faces—one human and one feline—symbolizing the duality of life and death, humanity and the supernatural.

The Fuente de Lavapatas, another highlight of the park, is a ceremonial site unlike anything else in the ancient Americas. This intricate network of carved channels, pools, and basins was etched directly into the bedrock of a riverbed, creating a sacred space where water and spirituality converge. The carvings include depictions of frogs, snakes, and human figures, all of which are thought to have played a role in rituals related to fertility, healing, and the cycle of life. Standing by the Fuente de Lavapatas, with the sound of water flowing over ancient carvings, it's easy to feel a profound connection to the people who once worshipped here.

The Bosque de las Estatuas, or Forest of Statues, offers a more immersive experience as visitors walk through a lush forest dotted with dozens of sculptures. This area provides a sense of how the statues might have originally appeared in their natural settings, surrounded by the dense vegetation of the Andean foothills. The statues in the forest vary in size and style, with some towering over three meters tall and others more modest in scale. Many depict warriors, deities, or hybrid creatures that seem to straddle the line between the human and the divine. The interplay of nature and art in this setting creates an atmosphere of mystery and wonder, as though the statues are sentinels watching over the forest.

While much about the San Agustín culture remains unknown, archaeologists have pieced together some details about their society through the study of these monuments. The statues and burial sites suggest a highly stratified society with a strong emphasis on ancestor worship and the afterlife. The tombs, often elaborately constructed and adorned, indicate that the elite members of society were buried with great care, accompanied by offerings and symbols of their status. The recurring motifs of animals and supernatural beings in the carvings hint at a belief system rooted in animism and shamanism, where the natural and spiritual worlds were deeply interconnected.

One of the enduring mysteries of San Agustín is the identity of the people who created these masterpieces. Unlike the Maya or the Inca, the San Agustín culture left no written records, and their language, customs, and even their name have been lost to time. The civilization appears to have flourished for several centuries before gradually declining, possibly due to environmental changes, conflict, or migration. The statues, however, remain as a testament to their ingenuity and spiritual depth, inviting visitors to ponder the mysteries of their lives and beliefs.

The preservation of San Agustín Archaeological Park is a testament to Colombia's commitment to protecting its cultural heritage. The site was first brought to international attention in the 18th and 19th centuries by travelers and explorers, and efforts to study and conserve it began in earnest in the 20th century. Today, the park is managed by the Colombian Institute of Anthropology and History, which works to ensure that the statues and monuments are safeguarded for future generations. Visitors are encouraged to respect the site by following established paths, avoiding contact with the sculptures, and appreciating the park's significance as a sacred and historical space.

Beyond the archaeological park itself, the surrounding town of San Agustín offers a charming base for further exploration. The town is known for its friendly atmosphere, traditional architecture, and vibrant markets where visitors can sample local cuisine and purchase handicrafts. Horseback riding and hiking are popular activities in the area, with trails leading to nearby waterfalls, viewpoints, and other archaeological sites such as Alto de los Ídolos and Alto de las Piedras. These satellite sites, though smaller than the main park, provide additional insights into the culture and artistry of the region.

Visiting San Agustín Archaeological Park is a deeply rewarding experience, one that combines the thrill of discovery with the serenity of a place steeped in history and spirituality. The statues, with their enigmatic expressions and intricate designs, offer a window into a world that is at once distant and strangely familiar. They remind us of the universality of human creativity and the enduring power of art to transcend time and connect us to the past. As you walk among these ancient monuments, surrounded by the beauty of the Andean landscape, you can't help but feel a sense of wonder and curiosity about the people who created them and the mysteries they left behind.

The park is more than just an archaeological site; it is a bridge between the past and the present, a place where history, art, and nature come together in perfect harmony. For those who venture to San Agustín, the journey is not just a physical one but also an intellectual and emotional exploration of Colombia's ancient heritage. Whether you're marveling at the artistry of a stone carving, contemplating the rituals once performed at the Fuente de Lavapatas, or simply soaking in the tranquility of the forest, San Agustín Archaeological Park offers an experience that lingers long after you leave, sparking a deeper appreciation for the richness and complexity of human history.

# Villa de Leyva: Colombia's Colonial Time Capsule

Nestled in the heart of Colombia's Boyacá department, Villa de Leyva stands as one of the country's most enchanting and best-preserved colonial towns. Walking through its cobblestone streets often feels like stepping back in time. Founded in 1572 by Hernán Suárez de Villalobos under Spanish rule, this small town has retained its historical charm, making it a cultural treasure and a favorite destination for travelers. Its pristine whitewashed buildings, red-tiled roofs, wooden balconies, and expansive Plaza Mayor reflect the architectural legacy of its colonial past. But Villa de Leyva is more than a relic of history; it is a living, breathing town where history, culture, and nature converge to create an experience that is as immersive as it is unforgettable.

The town's centerpiece is the massive Plaza Mayor, one of the largest cobblestone squares in South America, spanning an impressive 14,000 square meters. This vast, open space serves as both the physical and symbolic heart of Villa de Leyva. Surrounded by elegant colonial buildings, the square comes alive with the hum of daily life—locals selling handicrafts, children playing, and visitors marveling at its sheer size and atmosphere. At its center stands a simple stone fountain, a nod to the town's heritage, as it was once a vital source of water for its residents. Overlooking the plaza is the Iglesia Parroquial, a stately church whose white facade and bell tower dominate the scene, offering a glimpse into the town's religious traditions that have endured for centuries.

Exploring the streets radiating from the plaza reveals the town's commitment to preserving its colonial architecture. Unlike many other places where modern structures have replaced historical ones, Villa de Leyva has maintained a strict preservation policy. Its buildings remain true to their original design, with heavy wooden doors, wrought-iron details, and terracotta roofs. Many of these structures house boutique hotels, artisan shops, and family-run restaurants, blending history with contemporary uses in a way that feels authentic and respectful of the past. Strolling through the streets, you'll find surprises around every corner, whether it's a charming courtyard adorned with flowers or a small gallery showcasing local art.

Beyond its architectural beauty, Villa de Leyva is steeped in history and culture that extend far beyond its colonial origins. The area surrounding the town is rich in paleontological significance, with fossils that date back to the Cretaceous period, when this region was submerged under an ancient sea. The Museo Paleontológico, housed in a former monastery just outside the town, displays an impressive collection of fossils, including ammonites, marine reptiles, and the remains of a massive kronosaurus, a prehistoric marine predator. For those fascinated by paleontology, this museum provides a unique opportunity to connect with Colombia's ancient past.

A short drive from the town center leads to another remarkable site: El Fósil, a small museum built around the nearly complete skeleton of a kronosaurus, discovered in the area in 1977. Measuring over seven meters long, this fossil is one of the most complete specimens of its kind in the world. Visitors can marvel at its sheer size and imagine the prehistoric world that once existed here. The surrounding region is dotted with other fossil-rich sites, evidence of the area's geological history as an ancient seabed.

Villa de Leyva's historical significance extends to its role in Colombia's fight for independence. The nearby Casa Terracota, an extraordinary earthen structure often described as the "largest piece of pottery in the world," showcases the creativity and ingenuity of modern Colombian artisans. Built entirely from clay and fired in the sun, this architectural marvel blends art, sustainability, and functionality, serving as a symbol of how the town continues to innovate while honoring its roots.

For history enthusiasts, the Casa Museo Antonio Nariño provides a deeper dive into Colombia's struggle for independence. Antonio Nariño, known as the "Precursor of Independence," lived in Villa de Leyva and played a key role in translating and disseminating the Declaration of the Rights of Man and of the Citizen, a revolutionary document that inspired the fight for freedom across Latin America. The museum, located in his former home, features artifacts, documents, and exhibits that narrate his life and contributions to Colombia's independence movement.

Nature lovers will find plenty to explore in the surrounding landscapes, which are as captivating as the town itself. The desert-like terrain of the nearby Pozos Azules, or Blue Wells, offers a stark contrast to the lush greenery of the Andean highlands. These striking turquoise pools, created by mineral deposits, are a popular spot for hiking and photography. The surreal beauty of the Pozos Azules feels almost otherworldly, with their vibrant colors standing out against the arid backdrop.

Another natural wonder close to Villa de Leyva is the Iguaque National Park, a protected area known for its high-altitude ecosystems and biodiversity. The park is home to the sacred Iguaque Lagoon, which holds deep significance in Muisca mythology. According to legend, this lagoon is the cradle of humanity, as it is said that Bachué, the mother of the Muisca people, emerged from its waters. Hiking to the lagoon is a challenging but rewarding experience, taking visitors through páramo landscapes unique to the Andes. The trail winds through misty forests and open grasslands, offering sweeping views of the surrounding valleys before reaching the lagoon, which exudes a serene and mystical atmosphere.

Villa de Leyva is also renowned for its festivals, which reflect the town's vibrant culture and community spirit. One of the most famous is the Festival de Luces, or Festival of Lights, held in December. During this event, the town is illuminated with thousands of candles, creating a magical ambiance as residents and visitors celebrate the holiday season with music, fireworks, and traditional food. Another highlight is the Kite Festival, held in August, when the skies above Villa de Leyva are filled with colorful kites of all shapes and sizes. This event brings together families, artists, and kite enthusiasts from across Colombia, transforming the town into a lively celebration of creativity and tradition.

The culinary scene in Villa de Leyva is a delightful blend of traditional Boyacá flavors and contemporary Colombian cuisine. Local specialties include ajiaco, a hearty soup made with chicken, potatoes, and corn, and cuchuco de trigo, a wheat-based soup often served with pork or beef. Many restaurants in town offer these dishes alongside modern interpretations, using locally sourced ingredients to create a farm-to-table experience. The town is also known for its artisan bread, which is baked in traditional wood-fired ovens and pairs perfectly with cheese and coffee from the region.

For those seeking relaxation, the town's boutique hotels and guesthouses provide charming accommodations that reflect the character of Villa de Leyva. Many are set in restored colonial buildings, with courtyards filled with flowers, fountains, and hammocks that invite guests to unwind. These spaces blend comfort with history, offering a tranquil retreat after a day of exploration.

Villa de Leyva is more than just a colonial town frozen in time; it's a place where history, culture, nature, and community come together in harmony. Its cobblestone streets and whitewashed buildings preserve the essence of its past, while its festivals, museums, and natural attractions offer a dynamic and multifaceted experience. Whether you're wandering through the Plaza Mayor, marveling at prehistoric fossils, hiking to the Iguaque Lagoon, or simply savoring a freshly baked arepa in a quiet courtyard, Villa de Leyva invites you to slow down and appreciate the beauty of a place where time seems to stand still.

## Mompox: A Riverside Town Frozen in Time

Mompox, officially known as Santa Cruz de Mompox, is a town where time seems to have gently paused, preserving its colonial elegance and tranquil ambiance. Situated on an island in the Magdalena River, this riverside gem in Colombia's

Bolívar department feels like a place from another era, untouched by the hurried pace of modern life. Declared a UNESCO World Heritage Site in 1995, Mompox is a living museum of Spanish colonial architecture, yet it is far from being a static relic. It is a vibrant town with a deep connection to its history, culture, and the river that has sustained its people for centuries. Its blend of historical significance, architectural beauty, and serene atmosphere makes it a destination that captivates all who visit.

The journey to Mompox begins with a sense of adventure. Reaching this remote town requires a combination of road and river travel, as its location on an island in the Magdalena River has kept it isolated for much of its history. This isolation, however, is part of what has allowed Mompox to retain its authenticity and character. As you approach the town, the landscape shifts to reveal a patchwork of wetlands, lush vegetation, and waterways that hint at the town's historical importance as a trading hub. Mompox once played a crucial role in Colombia's colonial economy, serving as a key port for goods transported along the Magdalena River. Though its prominence waned with the rise of other ports, its legacy endures in its well-preserved streets and buildings.

The heart of Mompox is its historic center, a labyrinth of cobblestone streets lined with whitewashed colonial houses adorned with intricately wrought iron balconies and colorful wooden doors. The architecture here tells the story of a prosperous past, when wealthy families built grand homes to showcase their status. Many of these houses feature spacious courtyards filled with tropical plants and fountains, offering a cool respite from the heat. Walking through these streets is an experience that awakens the senses—the sound of horse hooves on cobblestones, the scent of blooming flowers, and the sight of the Magdalena River glimmering in the distance.

At the center of town is the Plaza de la Concepción, where the imposing Iglesia de Santa Bárbara stands as a symbol of Mompox's colonial heritage. This 17th-century church, with its intricate baroque facade and distinctive bell tower, is one of the most photographed landmarks in the town. Its location along the riverbank adds to its charm, as does the way its reflection dances on the water during sunrise and sunset. Stepping inside, visitors are greeted by a sense of history and reverence, with the church's wooden altars, religious statues, and centuries-old artwork serving as reminders of Mompox's deep spiritual roots.

The town's connection to religion is further evident in its many other churches, each with its own unique character. The Iglesia de San Francisco, with its simple yet elegant design, and the Iglesia de San Juan de Dios, which now houses a cultural center, are just two examples of the town's rich ecclesiastical architecture. These churches are not just historical landmarks; they are active places of worship where locals gather for mass, processions, and festivals. One of the most important events in Mompox is Semana Santa, or Holy Week, during which the town comes alive with elaborate religious ceremonies, processions, and music. This celebration, deeply rooted in tradition, attracts visitors from across Colombia and beyond.

Mompox's cultural heritage extends beyond its architecture and religious traditions. The town is renowned for its filigree jewelry, a delicate art form that has been passed down through generations. Filigree, or filigrana, involves crafting intricate designs from fine threads of gold or silver, resulting in jewelry that is both exquisite and lightweight. Workshops throughout Mompox offer visitors the chance to watch artisans at work, their hands deftly shaping metal into earrings, necklaces, and bracelets that are as much works of art as they are accessories. Purchasing a piece of filigree jewelry not only provides a beautiful keepsake but also supports the local economy and helps preserve this traditional craft.

The Magdalena River is the lifeblood of Mompox, shaping its history, economy, and daily life. In the early mornings, fishermen can be seen casting their nets into the water, continuing practices that have sustained their families for generations. The river also serves as a source of inspiration for local artists and musicians, whose work often reflects the rhythms and beauty of life along its banks. Boat tours offer a peaceful way to explore the river and its surrounding wetlands, providing opportunities to spot wildlife such as herons, iguanas, and even the elusive manatee. The tranquility of the river, combined with the soft sounds of nature, creates an atmosphere of serenity that is unique to Mompox.

The culinary scene in Mompox is a reflection of its riverside location and cultural heritage. Traditional dishes often feature fresh fish, prepared with local ingredients and spices that highlight the flavors of the region. Mojarra frita (fried fish) served with coconut rice and patacones (fried green plantains) is a staple, as is sancocho, a hearty soup made with fish, yucca, and plantains. Street vendors offer treats such as arepas de huevo (fried corn cakes stuffed with egg) and queso de capa, a local cheese with a distinctive flavor and texture. Meals in Mompox are often accompanied by refreshing drinks like limonada de panela, made with lime and unrefined cane sugar, or a chilled beer enjoyed along the riverbank.

For those seeking a deeper understanding of Mompox's history, the Casa de la Cultura is an essential stop. This cultural center and museum houses exhibits on the town's colonial past, its role in Colombia's independence, and its artistic traditions. One of the most notable figures associated with Mompox is Simón Bolívar, who famously declared, "If to Caracas I owe my life, then to Mompox I owe my glory." The town provided critical support to Bolívar's fight for independence, and its residents' contributions are celebrated in the museum's displays. Walking through these exhibits, visitors can gain a greater appreciation for Mompox's place in Colombia's history.

Mompox is not just a destination for history and culture; it is also a place to slow down and savor the simple pleasures of life. The town's laid-back pace invites visitors to linger, whether it's enjoying a cup of coffee in a shaded courtyard, watching the sunset over the river, or listening to the melodies of vallenato music drifting through the streets. The warmth and hospitality of the Mompoxinos, as the locals are known, add to the town's charm, making every interaction feel like a genuine connection.

Accommodations in Mompox range from boutique hotels housed in colonial mansions to cozy guesthouses that offer a more intimate experience. Many of these places maintain the town's historical character while providing modern comforts, such as air-conditioning and Wi-Fi, to ensure a pleasant stay. Staying overnight allows visitors to experience the town's magical ambiance after the day-trippers have left, when the streets are quiet, and the glow of lanterns illuminates the cobblestones.

Exploring Mompox is a journey into the soul of a town that has preserved its identity through centuries of change. Its architecture, traditions, and natural beauty offer a glimpse into a way of life that has endured, even as the world around it has evolved. For travelers seeking an authentic and enriching experience, Mompox provides a rare opportunity to step off the beaten path and discover a place where history and tranquility intertwine. Every moment spent in this riverside town is a reminder of the timeless beauty of Colombia's heritage, and the memories made here linger long after the journey ends.

## The Tatacoa Desert: Stargazing and Unique Landscapes

Stretching across the Huila department in central Colombia, the Tatacoa Desert is a striking expanse of arid beauty, a place where time and nature have sculpted a surreal and otherworldly landscape. Despite its name, the Tatacoa is not technically a desert but a tropical dry forest, characterized by its dramatic terrain of red and gray canyons, labyrinthine rock formations, and sparse vegetation. This unique environment, shaped by centuries of erosion, offers an experience unlike any other in Colombia. Beyond its breathtaking landscapes, the Tatacoa is also one of the best places in the country—and perhaps the entire continent—for stargazing, thanks to its minimal light pollution and clear skies. A visit to this captivating region combines the opportunity to explore its rugged terrain by day and gaze into the infinite cosmos by night.

The journey to the Tatacoa Desert begins with a sense of anticipation, as the scenery gradually shifts from lush green hills to the ochre and gray tones of this semi-arid landscape. Located about 40 kilometers from the city of Neiva, the Tatacoa is easily accessible by road, yet it feels like a remote frontier far removed from the bustling cities of Colombia. As you approach, the first glimpse of the desert's undulating terrain hints at the wonder that awaits. The red and gray hues of the landscape, interspersed with cacti and other hardy plants, create a stark and mesmerizing contrast against the blue sky.

The desert is divided into two main areas, each with its own distinct character. The first, known as El Cuzco, is famous for its red earth and labyrinth-like formations. Walking through this section feels like stepping into a natural maze, with narrow paths winding between towering walls of clay. The textures and patterns of the rock, shaped by wind and rain over thousands of years, are a testament to the power of erosion. Some formations resemble castles, towers, or even mythical creatures, sparking the imagination as you explore. The silence here is profound, broken only by the occasional rustle of wind or the chirp of a bird, adding to the sense of solitude and wonder.

In contrast, the second area, Los Hoyos, is characterized by its gray tones and more open terrain. This section has a lunar quality, with its cracked earth and sparse vegetation evoking images of an alien planet. The formations here are less intricate but no less impressive, with sweeping vistas that stretch to the horizon. The interplay of light and shadow on the gray earth, especially during sunrise or sunset, creates a breathtaking spectacle that draws photographers and nature enthusiasts alike. Los Hoyos also features several natural pools, where visitors can cool off and relax in the midst of the desert's arid beauty.

Exploring the Tatacoa Desert is an adventure that invites curiosity and discovery. There are no paved roads or marked trails within the desert itself, adding to its untamed allure. Visitors can wander on foot, rent bicycles, or join guided tours to uncover its hidden corners and learn about its geological and ecological significance. Local guides, often residents of the nearby village of Villavieja, bring the desert to life with their knowledge of its history, flora, and fauna. They recount stories of how the Tatacoa was once a lush forest millions of years ago, home to an abundance of plant and animal life, as evidenced by the fossils that have been unearthed here.

One of the most remarkable aspects of the Tatacoa Desert is its biodiversity, which thrives despite the harsh conditions. Cacti dominate the landscape, their spiny forms adapted to conserve water in the arid environment. Among them, the towering cactus species known as *cereus* can reach heights of up to six meters, standing as sentinels in the desert's vast expanse. The fauna of the Tatacoa includes a variety of reptiles, such as iguanas and snakes, as well as birds like hawks, owls, and the elusive vermilion flycatcher, whose vibrant red plumage adds a splash of color to the muted tones of the desert.

As night falls, the Tatacoa transforms into an entirely different realm. The desert's dry climate and lack of light pollution make it a haven for stargazers and astronomers. On a clear night, the sky comes alive with countless stars, planets, and constellations, offering an awe-inspiring view of the universe. This is one of the few places where the Milky Way can be seen in all its splendor, stretching across the sky like a celestial river. The experience of lying under this canopy of stars, surrounded by the quietude of the desert, is both humbling and exhilarating, a reminder of our small place in the cosmos.

For those eager to delve deeper into the mysteries of the night sky, the Tatacoa Astronomical Observatory offers an educational and interactive experience. Located near the desert's entrance, the observatory hosts nightly sessions where visitors can learn about astronomy, identify constellations, and view celestial objects through telescopes. The guides, often passionate astronomers themselves, provide fascinating insights into the science and mythology of the stars, making the experience both informative and magical. Whether you're a seasoned stargazer or a curious beginner, the observatory offers a unique opportunity to connect with the cosmos in a way that feels both personal and universal.

The Tatacoa Desert is also steeped in cultural significance, with its name derived from the word "tatacoa," which refers to a type of rattlesnake once common in the region. The name reflects the indigenous heritage of the area, as the desert was historically inhabited by indigenous peoples who revered its natural beauty and resources. Today, the nearby village of Villavieja serves as the gateway to the desert, offering a glimpse into the local way of life. The villagers, many of whom are descendants of the region's original inhabitants, are known for their hospitality and pride in their heritage. A visit to Villavieja's Paleontological Museum provides additional context, showcasing fossils and artifacts that reveal the ancient history of the desert and its transformation over millennia.

For those seeking a deeper connection to the Tatacoa, spending a night in the desert is an unforgettable experience. Several eco-lodges and camping sites cater to visitors, offering accommodations that range from rustic tents to comfortable cabins. Falling asleep under a blanket of stars, with the sounds of the desert as your lullaby, is a moment of pure serenity. The absence of city lights and noise creates an environment that feels removed from the modern world, allowing you to fully immerse yourself in the rhythm of nature.

Practical considerations are essential when planning a trip to the Tatacoa Desert. The climate can be unforgiving, with daytime temperatures often exceeding 35°C (95°F). Visitors should come prepared with sun protection, including hats, sunglasses, and sunscreen, as well as plenty of water to stay hydrated. Comfortable walking shoes are a must, as the terrain can be uneven and rocky. While the desert's beauty is undeniable, respecting its fragility is equally important. Visitors are encouraged to follow Leave No Trace principles, avoiding littering and staying on established paths to minimize their impact on this delicate ecosystem.

The Tatacoa Desert is more than just a natural wonder; it is a place of profound contrasts and connections. Its harsh yet beautiful landscapes challenge our perceptions of life and resilience, while its star-filled skies remind us of the infinite possibilities of the universe. Whether you come to hike through its canyons, marvel at its geological formations, or simply lose yourself in the endless expanse of stars, the Tatacoa offers an experience that is as humbling as it is inspiring. It is a destination that stays with you long after you leave, a reminder of the enduring beauty and mystery of the natural world.

## Guatapé and the Rock of El Peñol: A Day Trip from Medellín

About two hours outside Medellín, nestled in the heart of Colombia's Antioquia department, lies the vibrant town of Guatapé and the towering marvel known as the Rock of El Peñol. This picturesque region is a favorite day trip destination for both locals and visitors, offering a perfect blend of natural beauty, cultural charm, and adrenaline-inducing adventure. With its brightly painted houses, cobblestone streets, and the breathtaking views from the top of the Rock of El Peñol, Guatapé provides an unforgettable escape from the bustling rhythm of city life. The journey to this enchanting destination is as rewarding as the experience itself, drawing travelers into a world where every corner bursts with color, history, and panoramic landscapes.

The drive from Medellín to Guatapé winds through lush green hills and valleys, with glimpses of small farms and grazing cattle along the way. The journey is a visual treat, offering a sense of the rural charm that defines much of Antioquia's countryside. Many travelers choose to stop at the quaint town of El Peñol before continuing to Guatapé. El Peñol is significant in its own right, as it was relocated in the 1970s when the area was flooded to create the massive Peñol-Guatapé Reservoir. The original town now lies submerged beneath the shimmering waters, but the new El Peñol retains its historical essence and serves as a gateway to the region's attractions.

The Rock of El Peñol, or La Piedra del Peñol, dominates the landscape long before you reach its base. This massive monolith, standing 220 meters tall, is a geological wonder that seems almost otherworldly as it rises starkly from the ground. Composed primarily of quartz, feldspar, and mica, the rock is estimated to be around 70 million years old. Its sheer size and unique formation make it a natural curiosity, but it's the opportunity to climb to its summit that draws visitors from near and far. A stairway of 740 steps zigzags up the side of the rock, offering an ascent that is both challenging and exhilarating. Each step brings a new perspective, with sweeping views of the surrounding reservoir and rolling hills growing more spectacular as you climb.

Reaching the top of the rock is a triumph that rewards your effort with one of the most breathtaking panoramas in Colombia. The Peñol-Guatapé Reservoir stretches out in every direction, its turquoise waters weaving around a maze of green islands and peninsulas. The view is a patchwork of vibrant colors, with the deep blue of the water contrasting against the lush greenery of the landscape. On clear days, the horizon seems to stretch infinitely, making it a prime spot for photography and quiet reflection. At the summit, a small viewing platform and a handful of shops allow visitors to savor the moment, whether by enjoying a refreshing drink or simply soaking in the scenery.

Descending the rock, the town of Guatapé awaits just a short drive away. Known as "the most colorful town in Colombia," Guatapé lives up to its reputation with its vividly painted houses adorned with intricate decorations called *zócalos*. These bas-relief panels line the lower portions of the buildings and depict a variety of scenes, from pastoral landscapes to folkloric motifs and even abstract designs. Each *zócalo* tells a story, reflecting the identity, history, or daily life of the family that resides within. Walking through Guatapé feels like stepping into a living art gallery, where every street and façade is a canvas bursting with creativity and tradition.

The heart of Guatapé is its central plaza, Plaza de los Zócalos, a lively square surrounded by cafes, restaurants, and shops. The plaza's centerpiece is the Iglesia de Nuestra Señora del Carmen, a charming white and red church that adds to the town's picturesque allure. The square is a hub of activity, with vendors selling handmade crafts, musicians performing traditional Colombian tunes, and visitors enjoying the relaxed atmosphere. It's the perfect place to pause, sip on a cup of freshly brewed coffee, and watch the vibrant tapestry of life unfold around you.

A stroll along the Malecón, Guatapé's waterfront promenade, offers another perspective of the town's charm. The Malecón hugs the edge of the reservoir, providing stunning views of the water and surrounding hills. Here, visitors can rent kayaks or paddleboats to explore the reservoir up close, or simply enjoy a leisurely walk along the water's edge. The promenade is lined with food stalls and shops, offering everything from fresh fruit juices to souvenirs. The scent of sizzling *arepas* wafts through the air, tempting passersby to indulge in this classic Colombian street food.

For the more adventurous, the reservoir is a playground for water sports and outdoor activities. Jet skiing, wakeboarding, and paddleboarding are popular options, while boat tours offer a more relaxed way to explore the area. These tours often include a visit to the submerged ruins of El Peñol's old town, where the cross of a church steeple rises eerily above the water's surface. The reservoir itself is a testament to human ingenuity and adaptation, having transformed the region into a hub of tourism and recreation while providing hydroelectric power to much of Colombia.

While Guatapé is a destination that can be enjoyed in a single day, many visitors choose to extend their stay to fully appreciate its beauty and tranquility. The town offers a variety of accommodations, ranging from boutique hotels and guesthouses to eco-lodges nestled in the surrounding countryside. Staying overnight allows you to experience the town's quieter side, when the day-trippers have departed and the streets take on a more peaceful rhythm. At night, the lights of Guatapé reflect on the reservoir's calm waters, creating a magical ambiance that lingers in the memory.

Cultural immersion is another highlight of a visit to Guatapé. The town's residents, known as *guatapenses*, are known for their warmth and hospitality, welcoming visitors with open arms and a genuine pride in their heritage. Engaging with the locals provides insight into the traditions, stories, and way of life that make Guatapé so special. Many of the artisans who create the town's famous *zócalos* are happy to share their techniques and inspirations, offering a deeper appreciation for this unique art form.

Practical tips are essential for making the most of a trip to Guatapé and the Rock of El Peñol. Comfortable footwear is a must, especially if you plan to climb the rock, as the steps can be steep and uneven in places. Sunscreen, a hat, and plenty of water are also recommended, as the ascent is exposed to the sun. Arriving early is advisable, particularly on weekends or holidays when the site can become crowded. If possible, consider visiting on a weekday to enjoy a more relaxed and intimate experience.

The culinary scene in Guatapé is an integral part of the visit, offering a taste of Antioquian flavors and regional specialties. Many restaurants in town serve traditional dishes such as *bandeja paisa*, a hearty platter featuring beans, rice, chorizo, plantains, and avocado. Freshly caught fish from the reservoir, often grilled or fried, is another local favorite. For dessert, *obleas*—thin wafers filled with caramel, fruit jam, or condensed milk—are a sweet indulgence that pairs perfectly with coffee from the region's fertile hills.

Guatapé and the Rock of El Peñol embody the essence of what makes Colombia such a compelling destination: stunning natural landscapes, vibrant culture, and warm hospitality. Whether you're scaling the monolith for its unparalleled views, wandering the colorful streets of the town, or simply enjoying the serenity of the reservoir, this day trip offers an experience that is as enriching as it is unforgettable. It's a place where every step reveals something new, where history and modernity coexist in harmony, and where the beauty of Colombia shines in all its forms.

## The Pacific Coast: Whale Watching and Untouched Beaches

Colombia's Pacific Coast is a place where raw, untamed nature meets the rhythm of the ocean in one of the world's most biodiverse regions. Stretching from the Chocó department in the north to Nariño in the south, this coastline is a treasure trove of natural wonders, offering visitors a chance to connect with the wild in a way that few places can replicate. It's a land of dense rainforests, mangroves, black sand beaches, and crashing waves, where the air is alive with the calls of exotic birds and the distant splashes of breaching whales. With its remote location and minimal infrastructure, the Pacific Coast remains one of Colombia's best-kept secrets, a destination for those seeking both adventure and tranquility. Whale watching, in particular, has become a defining experience here, drawing travelers from across the globe to witness the majestic humpback whales that grace these waters each year.

Every year, from July to October, humpback whales undertake an extraordinary journey of more than 8,000 kilometers from the frigid waters of Antarctica to the warm, sheltered bays of Colombia's Pacific Coast. These gentle giants migrate to the region's shallow coastal waters to give birth and nurse their calves, making it one of the most significant whale nurseries in the world. The sight of a humpback breaching the surface, its massive body soaring into the air before crashing back down with a thunderous splash, is nothing short of awe-inspiring. Watching a mother whale teaching her calf to swim or hearing the hauntingly beautiful songs of the males underwater is a humbling reminder of the interconnectedness of life on Earth.

The small town of Bahía Solano, located in the Chocó department, is one of the best places to experience whale watching on Colombia's Pacific Coast. Surrounded by lush rainforest and accessible only by air or boat, Bahía Solano feels like a hidden paradise. From here, local guides organize boat tours that take visitors into the heart of the whales' breeding grounds. These tours are led by experienced boat operators who know the waters intimately and prioritize the safety and well-being of the whales. Observing these magnificent creatures in their natural habitat, without disrupting their behavior, is a deeply moving experience that leaves a lasting impression.

Nuquí, another gem of the Pacific Coast, offers a slightly different perspective for whale watching. This small, remote town is known for its pristine beaches and the warm hospitality of its Afro-Colombian and indigenous communities. The waters off Nuquí are teeming with marine life, and during whale season, it's common to spot humpbacks from the shore or while kayaking along the coastline. Guided boat tours provide an even closer look, allowing visitors to witness the whales' playful behavior up close. Nuquí also offers opportunities for snorkeling and diving, where you can explore vibrant coral reefs and encounter sea turtles, rays, and tropical fish, all while listening to the distant songs of the whales.

The whale watching experience on Colombia's Pacific Coast is not just about the whales themselves but also about the deep connection between the local communities and the marine environment. For many residents, the whales are more than just a tourist attraction—they are a symbol of the ocean's vitality and a source of cultural pride. Local guides often share stories and legends about the whales, weaving together science, tradition, and personal experience in a way that enriches the entire journey. Supporting these community-led initiatives helps ensure that whale watching in the region remains sustainable and respectful of the environment.

Beyond the whales, the Pacific Coast is home to some of the most untouched and stunning beaches in Colombia. Playa El Almejal, located near Bahía Solano, is a striking stretch of black sand framed by dense rainforest. The beach's dramatic beauty is enhanced by its wild, untamed nature, where waves crash against the shore with a powerful rhythm. Walking along El Almejal, you'll often have the beach entirely to yourself, with only the calls of birds and the sound of the ocean as your companions. The beach also serves as a nesting ground for sea turtles, and during nesting season, conservation programs allow visitors to participate in the release of baby turtles into the sea—a magical moment that underscores the importance of protecting these fragile ecosystems.

Farther south, Guachalito Beach near Nuquí offers another slice of paradise. This golden-sand beach is dotted with towering palm trees and dramatic rock formations, creating a postcard-perfect setting. Guachalito is ideal for those seeking solitude and relaxation, as its remote location ensures a sense of seclusion rarely found in more developed coastal destinations. The warm waters invite swimming and snorkeling, while the surrounding rainforest is perfect for hiking and exploring hidden waterfalls. Many eco-lodges in the area offer guided tours into the jungle, where you can learn about the region's incredible biodiversity and discover medicinal plants used by indigenous communities.

One of the most unique features of the Pacific Coast is its rich Afro-Colombian and indigenous heritage, which is deeply woven into the fabric of daily life. The region's music, dance, and cuisine reflect a vibrant blend of African, indigenous, and Spanish influences, creating a cultural tapestry as diverse as its natural environment. Traditional dishes such as *encocado*, a flavorful coconut-based seafood stew, and *arroz con piangua*, a dish made with a type of mangrove clam, showcase the bounty of the ocean and the ingenuity of local cooks. Meals are often accompanied by *viche*, a traditional fermented sugarcane drink that holds cultural significance for the Afro-Colombian communities.

The Pacific Coast's remoteness is both its greatest asset and its biggest challenge. Limited infrastructure means that accommodations are typically eco-lodges or small guesthouses, many of which are solar-powered and designed to minimize environmental impact. These lodgings offer a chance to disconnect from the modern world and immerse yourself in the rhythms of nature. Falling asleep to the sound of waves crashing on the shore and waking up to the calls of howler monkeys in the distance is an experience that stays with you long after you leave.

Getting to the Pacific Coast requires some planning, as most towns are accessible only by small planes from Medellín or Bogotá, or by boat from Buenaventura. The lack of direct road access adds to the region's sense of isolation, but it also helps preserve its pristine beauty. Visitors should come prepared for the region's tropical climate, which includes high humidity and frequent rain. Lightweight, quick-drying clothing, sturdy footwear, insect repellent, and a waterproof bag are essential items to pack. It's also important to respect the local environment and communities by following sustainable travel practices, such as reducing waste, supporting eco-friendly tour operators, and respecting wildlife.

The Pacific Coast is a destination that rewards those who venture off the beaten path. Its unparalleled natural beauty, combined with the chance to witness humpback whales in their element, creates an experience that is both exhilarating and deeply grounding. Whether you're standing on the deck of a boat as a whale breaches nearby, walking along an empty beach with the rainforest at your back, or sharing a meal with locals who welcome you like family, the Pacific Coast offers moments of wonder that are as unforgettable as they are transformative. It is a place where nature reigns supreme, where the ocean's power and mystery are palpable, and where the simple act of being present feels like a gift.

## Tierradentro: Colombia's Underground Tombs

Hidden deep within the verdant mountains of Colombia's Cauca department lies Tierradentro, a destination that offers one of the most enigmatic and fascinating archaeological experiences in South America. Known for its mysterious underground tombs, Tierradentro provides a rare glimpse into the ancient cultures that once thrived in this region. These tombs, dating from around 500 to 800 CE, are a testament to the ingenuity, artistry, and spiritual beliefs of the indigenous societies that created them. Declared a UNESCO World Heritage Site in 1995, Tierradentro is not only a place of historical significance but also one of profound natural beauty. The journey to this extraordinary site is as much about connecting with its hauntingly beautiful past as it is about immersing yourself in the breathtaking landscapes of the Andes.

Tierradentro is not the kind of place you stumble upon by accident. Located in a remote, mountainous region, getting there requires determination and a sense of adventure. Most visitors arrive via the town of San Andrés de Pisimbalá, which serves as the gateway to the archaeological park. The journey winds through rugged terrain, with roads cutting through mist-covered hills and valleys. The sense of isolation only adds to the mystique of Tierradentro, as though you are traveling back in time to a place where history lies hidden beneath the surface.

The main attraction of Tierradentro is its hypogea—underground burial chambers carved directly into the rock. These tombs, some of which are over nine meters deep, were used as collective burial sites for the elite members of the society that once inhabited this area. Accessed via steep, spiral staircases, the chambers are adorned with intricate paintings and carvings that reflect the spiritual beliefs and artistic sensibilities of their creators. The designs often mimic the interiors of houses, with geometric patterns, anthropomorphic figures, and depictions of animals thought to symbolize the connection between the living and the dead. The use of red, black, and white pigments adds a striking visual element, creating an atmosphere that is both somber and awe-inspiring.

Exploring the Tierradentro Archaeological Park is an immersive experience that takes you on a journey through five main sites: Alto de San Andrés, Alto de Segovia, Alto del Duende, El Tablón, and Alto del Aguacate. Each site offers a unique perspective on the ancient culture that created these tombs, with its own set of hypogea and artifacts. Alto de

Segovia is perhaps the most famous, with its well-preserved chambers and vivid wall paintings. Descending into these tombs is an almost otherworldly experience, as the cool air and dim light create an atmosphere of reverence and mystery. The carvings and paintings seem to whisper stories of a long-lost world, inviting visitors to ponder the beliefs and rituals of the people who once gathered here to honor their dead.

El Tablón, unlike the other sites, features a collection of stone statues rather than burial chambers. These statues, carved from volcanic rock, depict human figures with exaggerated features, such as large eyes and open mouths. Some hold objects such as staffs or bowls, suggesting their role as guardians or participants in ceremonial practices. The statues provide a fascinating contrast to the hypogea, offering a glimpse into the artistic diversity of the Tierradentro culture. They also raise intriguing questions about the society's use of symbolism and its relationship with the spiritual world.

The hike to Alto del Aguacate is a highlight for many visitors, combining archaeological discovery with stunning natural scenery. This site, perched on a ridge with sweeping views of the surrounding mountains, features dozens of tombs scattered along its slopes. The climb is challenging, but the reward is worth it—not only for the archaeological treasures but also for the sense of connection to the land and its history. Standing at the summit, with the wind carrying the scent of pine and the distant sound of birdsong, it's easy to imagine how this place might have been seen as sacred by those who built the tombs.

The significance of Tierradentro extends beyond its archaeological features. The site is also a testament to the resilience and creativity of the indigenous communities that have called this region home for centuries. The Paez people, descendants of the ancient Tierradentro culture, continue to live in the area, maintaining their traditions and spiritual practices. Engaging with the local community provides an opportunity to learn about their way of life and the enduring connection they feel to the land and its history. Many local guides are Paez themselves, offering insights that go beyond the surface to reveal the deeper meanings of the tombs and their symbolism.

Visiting Tierradentro is as much about the journey as it is about the destination. The region's natural beauty is a constant companion, with its rolling hills, dense forests, and crystal-clear streams creating a serene backdrop for exploration. The area is a haven for birdwatchers, with species such as the Andean cock-of-the-rock and the emerald toucanet frequently spotted among the trees. Hiking between the different sites offers a chance to immerse yourself in this rich biodiversity, with trails that wind through landscapes untouched by modern development. The sense of peace and solitude is profound, making Tierradentro a place where you can truly disconnect from the outside world.

Practical considerations are essential when planning a trip to Tierradentro. The remote location means that accommodations are limited to small guesthouses and family-run hostels in San Andrés de Pisimbalá. These lodgings are simple but comfortable, offering a warm welcome and a chance to experience the hospitality of the local community. Meals are typically home-cooked and feature traditional Colombian dishes, such as arepas, sancocho, and fresh fruit from the region. Visitors should come prepared for the physical demands of exploring the site, as the hikes can be steep and the tombs require navigating narrow staircases. Sturdy footwear, sunscreen, and plenty of water are essential, as is a sense of curiosity and adventure.

Conservation efforts play a crucial role in preserving Tierradentro for future generations. The tombs and statues are vulnerable to erosion, vandalism, and the effects of climate change, making it essential for visitors to respect the site and follow guidelines set by park authorities. Supporting local initiatives, such as hiring Paez guides and purchasing handicrafts made by the community, helps to ensure that the benefits of tourism are shared equitably and contribute to the preservation of this cultural treasure.

Tierradentro is more than just an archaeological site—it is a place where history, culture, and nature converge in a way that is both humbling and inspiring. The underground tombs, with their intricate designs and mysterious origins, offer a window into a world that is as fascinating as it is enigmatic. But beyond the artifacts and the sites themselves, it is the sense of connection—to the past, to the land, and to the people who have lived here for generations—that makes Tierradentro truly unforgettable. For those willing to venture off the beaten path, this hidden gem of Colombia offers an experience that lingers in the mind and heart long after the journey ends.

## Jardín: A Coffee Town with Vibrant Colors

Nestled in the lush, rolling hills of the Antioquia department, Jardín is a picture-perfect coffee town where tradition, natural beauty, and vibrant culture blend seamlessly. Known for its colorful colonial architecture, picturesque plazas, and the surrounding coffee plantations that have shaped its identity, Jardín offers an enchanting escape into the heart of Colombia's coffee-growing region. Unlike some of its more tourist-heavy counterparts, Jardín retains a sense of authenticity that charms visitors from the moment they arrive. It is a town where life moves at a slower pace, where the distant hum of coffee processing mingles with the sound of birdsong, and where every corner seems to tell a story of heritage and resilience.

The journey to Jardín is as much a part of the experience as the town itself. Located roughly three hours south of Medellín, the drive winds through breathtaking landscapes of emerald-green valleys and steep cliffs. The route offers glimpses of local life, with farmers tending to their crops and small roadside stalls selling fresh fruit and coffee. As you approach the town, the towering Andes provide a dramatic backdrop, giving way to a tranquil valley where Jardín lies tucked away like a hidden gem. The first sight of its colorful, orderly streets and iconic church spires feels like stepping into a postcard.

At the heart of Jardín is its central plaza, a vibrant hub that embodies the soul of the town. The Plaza El Libertador, as it is known, is surrounded by brightly painted buildings adorned with intricately carved wooden balconies. The plaza comes alive throughout the day, with locals gathering to chat over coffee, children playing, and vendors selling everything from fresh flowers to handmade crafts. Towering above it all is the Basílica Menor de la Inmaculada Concepción, an imposing neo-Gothic church constructed entirely of hand-carved stone. Its twin spires and intricate facade draw the eye, while the interior, with its soaring ceilings and stained-glass windows, offers a serene space for reflection.

The plaza's cafes are a cornerstone of life in Jardín and a must-visit for anyone exploring the town. Small tables spill onto the cobblestone streets, shaded by colorful umbrellas and the leafy canopy of towering trees. These cafes serve some of the finest coffee in Colombia, brewed from beans grown in the surrounding hills. Sipping a cup of freshly brewed coffee while watching the rhythms of daily life unfold is an experience that captures the essence of Jardín. It's not just about the coffee but about the connection to the land and the people who cultivate it with care.

Beyond the plaza, Jardín's streets are a feast for the eyes. The town is renowned for its vividly painted houses, each adorned with decorative wooden doors and floral displays that spill from balconies and windowsills. The colors are not chosen at random but are a reflection of the town's cultural heritage and the pride of its residents. Walking through these streets feels like wandering through an open-air art gallery, where every detail has been carefully considered. The interplay of colors, textures, and light creates a visual harmony that is both uplifting and inspiring.

Jardín's connection to coffee is evident at every turn, and no visit is complete without exploring the surrounding coffee farms. The fertile soil and mild climate of the region make it ideal for cultivating coffee, and many family-run fincas (coffee farms) welcome visitors to learn about the process from bean to cup. A tour of a coffee farm typically begins with a walk through the plantation, where rows of coffee plants stretch as far as the eye can see. Guides explain the nuances of coffee cultivation, from selecting the ripest cherries to the careful process of drying and roasting the beans. The experience often concludes with a tasting, where you can savor the distinct flavors of locally grown coffee and gain a deeper appreciation for the craftsmanship behind every cup.

For those seeking adventure, Jardín offers a wealth of outdoor activities that showcase its natural beauty. The surrounding countryside is crisscrossed with hiking trails that lead to stunning vistas, hidden waterfalls, and lush cloud forests. One of the most popular hikes is the trek to La Cueva del Esplendor, a breathtaking cave with a waterfall cascading through a hole in its roof. Reaching the cave requires a combination of hiking and horseback riding, but the effort is more than worth it. The sight of sunlight streaming through the opening and illuminating the rushing water below is a moment of pure magic.

Birdwatching is another highlight of Jardín, thanks to its location within one of the most biodiverse regions in the world. The town is particularly famous for its Andean cock-of-the-rock lek, a site where these vibrant, crimson-plumed birds gather for their elaborate mating displays. Early morning visits to the lek offer the chance to witness this extraordinary spectacle, as the males emit loud calls and perform acrobatic movements to attract a mate. The area around Jardín is also home to a variety of other bird species, including toucans, hummingbirds, and tanagers, making it a paradise for nature enthusiasts.

Jardín's cultural heritage is celebrated through its festivals and traditions, which provide a window into the town's vibrant community spirit. One of the most anticipated events is the Festival de las Flores y del Café, held annually to honor the region's two most iconic products. The festival features parades, live music, traditional dances, and exhibitions showcasing the artistry of local craftsmen and women. It's a time when the entire town comes together to celebrate its roots and share its culture with visitors. Even outside of festival season, the warmth and hospitality of Jardín's residents are evident in every interaction, from a friendly greeting on the street to the care taken in preparing a meal at a local eatery.

The culinary scene in Jardín is a reflection of its agricultural abundance and cultural traditions. Local restaurants and food stalls serve hearty, flavorful dishes that showcase the best of Antioquian cuisine. Bandeja paisa, a signature dish of the region, is a must-try, featuring a generous platter of beans, rice, chorizo, fried egg, avocado, and arepa. Other specialties include sancocho, a comforting soup made with meat, plantains, and yucca, and empanadas filled with savory meats and spices. For dessert, try a slice of guava paste paired with fresh cheese, a simple yet satisfying combination that highlights the region's tropical flavors.

Accommodations in Jardín range from charming boutique hotels to rustic guesthouses, many of which are housed in beautifully restored colonial buildings. Staying overnight allows visitors to experience the town's tranquil ambiance after the day-trippers have left. In the evening, the plaza takes on a different character, with the glow of lanterns reflecting off the cobblestones and the sound of live music drifting through the air. It's a time to relax, reflect, and savor the unique charm of this coffee town.

Jardín is more than just a destination—it's an invitation to slow down and connect with the essence of Colombia's coffee culture. Its vibrant colors, welcoming community, and stunning natural surroundings create a sense of harmony that is both invigorating and grounding. Whether you're sipping coffee in the plaza, exploring a coffee farm, or marveling at the beauty of a hidden waterfall, Jardín offers an experience that lingers in the heart and mind long after you've returned home. It's a place where the simple joys of life are celebrated, and where every moment feels like a masterpiece painted in the brightest colors.

# Leticia: Gateway to the Amazon

Leticia, a small yet vibrant town perched at the southernmost tip of Colombia, is the beating heart of the country's Amazon region. It serves as the primary gateway to one of the most biodiverse and awe-inspiring ecosystems on Earth: the Amazon rainforest. Bordering Brazil and Peru, Leticia is a confluence of cultures, languages, and natural wonders, offering travelers an entry point into the enigmatic world of the jungle. Far removed from Colombia's bustling urban centers, this remote town is a place where nature reigns supreme, and the rhythm of life is dictated by the flow of the Amazon River. For those seeking adventure, tranquility, or a deeper connection to the natural world, Leticia is the starting point of a journey unlike any other.

Reaching Leticia is an adventure in itself. The town is accessible only by air or river, with flights from Bogotá offering the most convenient route for visitors. As the plane descends, the view transforms into an endless sea of green, broken only by the winding silver ribbon of the Amazon River. The dense canopy of the rainforest stretches as far as the eye can see, a vast and untamed wilderness that holds secrets millions of years in the making. Upon landing at Alfredo Vásquez Cobo International Airport, the humid air and symphony of birdsong immediately signal your arrival in a world far removed from the chaos of modern life.

The first impression of Leticia is one of warmth—not just the tropical climate, but the welcoming spirit of its people. The town is home to a mix of cultures, including indigenous communities such as the Ticuna, Yagua, and Cocama, whose traditions and knowledge of the rainforest are deeply woven into the fabric of life here. Spanish is widely spoken, but it's not uncommon to hear Portuguese and indigenous languages in the streets, reflecting Leticia's unique position at the intersection of three countries. The town's central market is a microcosm of this diversity, bustling with vendors selling everything from tropical fruits and fresh fish to handmade crafts and traditional remedies.

Leticia's proximity to the Amazon River makes it a hub for river-based exploration, and no visit would be complete without venturing onto the water. The river, vast and powerful, is both a lifeline and a highway, connecting remote communities and providing access to the deeper reaches of the rainforest. Boat tours departing from Leticia offer a range of experiences, from short excursions to multi-day journeys that delve into the heart of the Amazon. As the boat glides along the water, the scenery shifts constantly—dense jungle on one side, small riverside settlements on the other, and the occasional splash of a pink river dolphin breaking the surface. These rare and playful creatures, known locally as *botos*, are a highlight for many visitors and a reminder of the river's extraordinary biodiversity.

One of the most popular destinations near Leticia is Isla de Los Micos, or Monkey Island, a sanctuary for hundreds of playful primates. Accessible by a short boat ride, the island is home to squirrel monkeys that are known for their curiosity and willingness to interact with visitors. As you step onto the island, the rustling of leaves and the chatter of monkeys create an atmosphere of excitement. The guides, often locals with deep ties to the land, share fascinating insights into the behavior and ecology of these energetic creatures. While the monkeys' antics are entertaining, this experience also underscores the importance of conservation and responsible tourism in protecting their habitat.

Farther along the river lies the Amacayacu National Park, a sprawling expanse of protected rainforest that showcases the Amazon's staggering diversity. Covering more than 4,000 square kilometers, the park is a haven for countless species of plants, animals, and insects, many of which are found nowhere else on Earth. Guided hikes through the park offer the chance to encounter wildlife such as sloths, toucans, and poison dart frogs, as well as towering trees that form the backbone of this ancient ecosystem. The Ticuna people, who inhabit the area, play an integral role in the park's conservation efforts, sharing their traditional knowledge with visitors and demonstrating how they live in harmony with the rainforest.

Another must-visit site is the Lago Tarapoto, a pristine lake located about an hour from Leticia. Surrounded by dense jungle, the lake is a peaceful retreat where visitors can swim, kayak, or simply relax while taking in the beauty of the Amazon. The waters of Lago Tarapoto are also home to pink river dolphins, and with a bit of patience, you may be rewarded with the unforgettable sight of these graceful creatures surfacing nearby. The lake is particularly enchanting at sunset, when the sky is painted in hues of orange and pink, reflecting off the still waters and creating a scene of unparalleled serenity.

The indigenous communities around Leticia are central to the region's identity and offer a unique opportunity for cultural exchange. Many communities welcome visitors to learn about their traditions, art, and way of life, providing insights that deepen your understanding of the Amazon and its people. The Ticuna, for example, are renowned for their intricate crafts, including woven baskets and colorful masks that are used in ceremonial dances. Spending time with these communities not only supports their livelihoods but also fosters a greater appreciation for the wisdom that has been passed down through generations. It's a chance to see the rainforest through their eyes, as a living entity that provides not just sustenance but also spiritual guidance.

Leticia itself, though small, has its own charms and points of interest. The Malecón, a riverside promenade, is a favorite spot for locals and visitors alike to enjoy the view of the Amazon River. In the evenings, the area comes alive with food stalls offering regional delicacies such as *pescado moqueado* (smoked fish) and *patacones* (fried green plantains). The town's main square, Parque Santander, is another highlight, especially at dusk when thousands of parakeets return to roost in the trees. The cacophony of their calls creates a spectacle that is both chaotic and mesmerizing, a reminder of the untamed spirit of the Amazon that permeates every aspect of life here.

Accommodations in Leticia range from budget hostels to eco-lodges that provide a more immersive experience of the rainforest. Many lodges are located just outside the town, surrounded by jungle and accessible only by boat. Staying at one of these lodges offers a chance to wake up to the sounds of the rainforest, with howler monkeys serving as your morning alarm and the scent of the jungle filling the air. These lodges often work closely with local communities, incorporating sustainable practices and offering guided tours that highlight the region's natural and cultural richness.

Practical considerations are important when planning a trip to Leticia and the Amazon. The climate is hot and humid year-round, so lightweight, breathable clothing is essential, along with sturdy footwear for jungle treks. Mosquito repellent and sunscreen are must-haves, as are waterproof bags to protect your belongings during boat rides. Travel in the Amazon requires a sense of flexibility and respect for the environment, as the weather can be unpredictable and the terrain challenging. However, the rewards far outweigh the challenges, offering experiences that are as unforgettable as they are transformative.

Leticia is more than just a gateway to the Amazon—it is a destination that encapsulates the wonder and complexity of this extraordinary region. From the vibrant culture of its indigenous communities to the breathtaking beauty of its natural landscapes, it is a place that leaves a lasting impression on all who visit. The Amazon is often described as the lungs of the Earth, and spending time in Leticia makes you keenly aware of its importance, not just for Colombia but for the entire planet. Whether you're cruising along the river, exploring the depths of the rainforest, or simply sitting beneath the vast canopy of stars, Leticia offers a journey into the heart of the wild—a journey that stays with you long after you've left its shores.

# CONCLUSION

## Recap: Why Colombia Should Be Your Next Adventure

Colombia is a country that defies expectations and redefines the very notion of adventure. Its landscapes stretch from the Caribbean's turquoise waters to the snow-capped peaks of the Andes, from the dense Amazon rainforest to the golden deserts of La Guajira. Its cities hum with energy and innovation, while its small towns preserve the traditions of centuries past. The diversity of experiences Colombia offers is unmatched, and what makes it even more remarkable is the warmth and resilience of its people. For adventurers, explorers, and those simply seeking a deeper connection to the world, Colombia is not just a destination—it's an invitation to uncover stories, challenge perceptions, and create memories that linger long after your journey ends.

The natural beauty of Colombia is staggering. Few places on Earth can match the variety of ecosystems packed into a single country. The Andes, with their dramatic peaks and verdant valleys, are home to some of the most rewarding hiking trails in South America. Treks like the Cocora Valley, where towering wax palms sway against a backdrop of misty mountains, or the ascent to the Lost City of the Tayrona, where ancient ruins emerge from the jungle, offer challenges that are as physically invigorating as they are spiritually fulfilling. For those drawn to the allure of water, the Caribbean coastline provides pristine beaches like those of Tayrona National Park, where golden sands meet lush rainforest, and the Pacific coast reveals a rugged beauty teeming with marine life, including migrating humpback whales. Meanwhile, the Amazon draws adventurers into its mysterious depths, offering encounters with rare wildlife and a chance to connect with the indigenous cultures that have called the rainforest home for millennia.

Colombia's cities are a dynamic reflection of its history and its future, each offering something distinct. Bogotá, the sprawling capital, is the cultural and intellectual heart of the nation. Its museums, such as the Gold Museum and the Botero Museum, house treasures that tell the story of Colombia's rich heritage. The vibrant district of La Candelaria, with its colonial architecture and colorful murals, invites exploration, while Monserrate offers a panoramic view of the city's vast expanse. Medellín, once plagued by its troubled past, has emerged as a beacon of transformation. The city's innovative approach to urban planning is evident in its cable cars that connect hillside neighborhoods, its lush parks, and its thriving arts scene. Cartagena, with its walled city and Caribbean charm, is a vivid reminder of Colombia's colonial past, while Cali pulses to the rhythm of salsa, embodying the infectious energy of the Colombian people.

What truly sets Colombia apart, however, is its people. Colombians are some of the most welcoming and hospitable individuals you will ever meet, eager to share their culture, stories, and traditions. This warmth is palpable whether you're wandering through the streets of a bustling city or sipping coffee in a small Andean village. It's in the smiles of artisans proudly showing their crafts, the enthusiasm of guides sharing the secrets of their land, and the shared laughter over a meal of local favorites like *bandeja paisa* or *ajiaco*. Every interaction feels genuine, leaving visitors not just with memories of beautiful places but with connections to the people who make those places special.

Colombia's culinary scene is as diverse as its landscapes. Each region offers its own flavors and specialties, reflecting the unique blend of indigenous, African, and Spanish influences that shape the country's identity. In the coffee region, the aroma of freshly brewed coffee is ever-present, and tours of fincas reveal the care and passion behind every cup. Along the coasts, seafood reigns supreme, with dishes like coconut rice and *encocado* (a coconut-based seafood stew) highlighting the bounty of the ocean. In the highlands, hearty meals such as *lechona*—slow-roasted pork stuffed with rice and peas—

offer a taste of tradition. Street food, from *arepas* to *empanadas*, provides an opportunity to savor Colombia's flavors on the go, while fruit markets burst with tropical delights like lulo, guanabana, and maracuyá.

Adventure seekers find no shortage of thrills in Colombia. The country's varied terrain makes it a paradise for outdoor enthusiasts, whether you're scaling the peaks of the Sierra Nevada, rafting down the rapids of the Magdalena River, or paragliding over the coffee-covered hills of Antioquia. Diving enthusiasts can explore underwater worlds off the coast of San Andrés and Providencia, while birdwatchers revel in the fact that Colombia boasts more bird species than any other country in the world. For those who prefer a more relaxed pace, horseback riding through the rolling landscapes of Boyacá or simply strolling through the colorful streets of towns like Jardín and Barichara offers a chance to connect with nature and tradition in equal measure.

Colombia's cultural festivals are another draw, showcasing the country's vibrant spirit and deep-rooted traditions. The Carnival of Barranquilla, a UNESCO-recognized event, is a riot of color, music, and dance, bringing together communities in a celebration of life. Medellín's Flower Festival transforms the city into a sea of blooms, while Cali's Feria de Cali is a testament to the city's love of salsa. Each festival is an opportunity to experience Colombia's culture at its most exuberant, where the line between participant and spectator blurs, and everyone is invited to join in the celebration.

What makes Colombia truly remarkable is how its people have embraced their history and used it as a foundation for growth and resilience. The country has faced its share of challenges, but rather than being defined by them, Colombians have transformed adversity into opportunity. This spirit of renewal is evident in Medellín's metamorphosis, in the thriving ecotourism initiatives that protect its natural resources, and in the way its people approach life with optimism and determination. Traveling through Colombia is not just about seeing beautiful places—it's about witnessing a story of transformation and hope.

Practical considerations make Colombia an increasingly accessible destination for travelers. Its infrastructure has improved significantly in recent years, with modern airports, reliable transportation options, and a growing number of eco-friendly lodges and boutique hotels catering to a range of budgets. Safety, once a concern for visitors, has improved dramatically, and while it's always wise to exercise caution and stay informed, Colombia today is a welcoming and hospitable place for travelers from around the globe. The country's growing reputation as a must-visit destination has led to an increase in direct flights, making it easier than ever to reach its major cities and regions.

Colombia's appeal lies in its ability to offer something for everyone. Whether you're a history buff wandering the cobblestone streets of Villa de Leyva, a nature lover trekking through the Amazon, or a foodie sampling dishes in a bustling market, the country's diversity ensures that every traveler finds their own connection to its rich tapestry. It's a place where contrasts coexist harmoniously: ancient traditions meet modern innovation, bustling cities give way to tranquil countryside, and adventure intertwines with relaxation. The sheer variety of experiences available makes Colombia a destination that can be explored multiple times, with each visit revealing a new layer of its complex and captivating identity.

The magic of Colombia is not just in its landscapes or its cities, but in the way it makes you feel. It's the sense of discovery as you uncover hidden gems, the warmth of a stranger's smile, and the realization that you're part of a story much larger than yourself. Colombia is not just a destination to check off a list; it's a place that stays with you, where the memories you make are infused with a vibrancy and depth that only this country can provide. For anyone seeking adventure, connection, and a deeper understanding of the world, Colombia is waiting to be discovered. It's not just a place to visit—it's a place to experience, a place to feel, and a place to remember.

# BONUS 1: PRINTABLE TRAVEL JOURNAL

# BONUS 2: 10 TIPS "THAT CAN SAVE THE DAY" ON YOUR TRIP IN COLOMBIA

# BONUS 3: ESSENTIAL PHRASES FOR YOUR DAILY TRAVEL NEEDS IN COLOMBIA

Printed in Great Britain
by Amazon